BROTHERS OF MEN

RENÉ VOILLAUME

Brothers of Men

LETTERS TO THE PETITS FRÈRES

Edited, with an Introduction,
by Lancelot Sheppard

BALTIMORE
HELICON PRESS

This translation of extracts from *Letters aux fraternités*, (two volumes, Paris, Éditions du Cerf, 1960), was made by A. MANSON

This edition first published in 1966
by Helicon Press, Inc.
1120 N. Calvert Street, Baltimore, Maryland 21202
Reprinted in 1967
Library of Congress Catalog Card Number 66–17082
© 1966 Darton, Longman and Todd Ltd.

Nihil Obstat Joannes M. T. Barton STD, LSS, censor deputatus.   Imprimatur ✠ Patritius J. Casey Vic. Gen., Westmonasterii, die 18 Aprilis 1966

Printed in Great Britain by
Richard Clay (The Chaucer Press), Ltd., Bungay, Suffolk

CONTENTS

INTRODUCTION

When, nearly half a century ago, Fr. Charles de Foucauld died at the hands of marauders before the doors of his little hermitage in the Sahara, he died alone and in silence; he seemed to die a failure. His death was in some sort a symbolic summary of his life as a hermit in the desert. At least it was the crowning proof of the falsity of that remark of an Arab's to Ernest Psichari: 'You Frenchmen, you possess the kingdom of earth; we, the Arabs, possess the kingdom of heaven.'

His life is today too well known for it to be recounted in detail all over again. Here a short summary must suffice. It is necessary to know that he was born in 1858—in a house in Strasbourg that is now the Banque de France and in which the *Marseillaise* was first sung by its author, Rouget de Lisle—and that he died in 1916. To put it like that is a way of saying that he belonged to another epoch, that he lived and died under conditions far different from our own; his preoccupations, his difficulties, the advantages that he enjoyed, the very material circumstances of his life, would seem to have nothing in common with our times, and, in fact, looking at it thus one is tempted to say that really this somewhat eccentric figure, this part soldier, part monk, part hermit, and part intelligence agent has nothing to say to us, has no message for our time. Yet to judge by certain manifestations of this second half of the twentieth century he still seems to speak clearly to modern men and women.

He was brought up by his grandfather, and after schooling in Nantes managed to get into the military academy at St. Cyr with the object of a commission in the cavalry. Both at

St. Cyr and afterwards he created something of a name for himself by his wild escapades and lack of discipline; in Algeria, things came to a head, for his mistress had preceded him there and was giving herself out as the Vicomtesse de Foucauld. When the regiment arrived his colonel told him that he must send her home at once. His only reply was that, since she was not under military discipline, she was free to do as she liked, and that as he only visited her in his free time his work did not suffer on that account. He was removed from the active list for notoriously bad conduct, and thereupon retired with the cause of the trouble to the shores of the Lake of Geneva. At this point his story might have become commonplace. He had money and he was not particularly enamoured of peacetime soldiering. Yet this year formed one of the turning-points of his life.

When an insurrection broke out in Africa he applied to be reinstated, and saw service in Algeria. At the end of the campaign he asked for a period of leave in order to undertake a journey of exploration in southern Algeria. His request was refused and, impetuous as ever, he resigned his commission on the spot. He was then twenty-three. He now settled in Algeria and for nearly two years worked hard in preparation for a more ambitious project. He studied Arabic and Hebrew, and when he set out into the interior of Morocco he was able to do so disguised as a Jewish rabbi. He took with him as his guide the rabbi who had been his Hebrew tutor, and for the best part of a year they were lost 'somewhere in Morocco'. At that time, it has to be realised, Morocco was to all intents and purposes a closed country to Europeans. We cannot linger on the dangers and the very great hardships de Foucauld endured during this journey, nor on the dangers that he encountered. They were by no means inconsiderable. It is necessary to point out, though, that the endurance and singleness of purpose displayed by the young officer were proof of at least a changed attitude of mind.

On the results of this journey the Paris Geographical Society awarded Charles de Foucauld its gold medal, for he had mapped out upwards of a thousand miles of previously unexplored territory in Morocco, and had added some three thousand heights to the maps in place of the few dozen that were known before his journey. He returned now to Paris and wrote a book recording the results of his exploration. His life now was very different from that of his earlier years and his time in the army. He rarely went out, but spent all his time at his books. Occasionally he would visit his sister, and at her house met some of her friends.

The solitude in Africa, the contact with Jews and Mohammedans, the sight of people with a religion which seemed to penetrate their whole lives, the piety of his sister and her friends, all helped to revive in him the germ of that faith which seemed no longer his. He began to haunt the Paris churches, the same strange prayer always on his lips: 'My God, if you exist, grant me to know you!' At his sister's house he met Abbé Huvelin, curate at the church of St. Augustine in Paris, a priest much sought after as a confessor and with a reputation as a preacher.

One morning towards the end of October 1886 de Foucauld was in St. Augustine's. Some instinctive movement took him to Abbé Huvelin's confessional. 'I have not come to confession,' murmured this strange penitent; 'I have no faith.' A few questions deftly put and the position was made abundantly clear to the Abbé. 'It is not your faith that is at fault, my friend,' he urged. 'It is your conscience; you must purify it.' More questions. The whole sorry past was gone through, and de Foucauld received absolution, the first since the days of his boyhood.

There were no half measures about de Foucauld. As with his pleasures in early life, as with his exploring, now with his refound religion. In quick succession he made four retreats to know what was the will of God for him. Abbé Huvelin had to restrain him somewhat, for this new and terrible penitent was a man with a will of iron. He was resolved to live the gospel to the letter.

He looked about him to find the life that was the hardest and poorest, the most like that of the Holy Family at Nazareth. He found it, for a time at least, with the Trappist monks at the abbey of our Lady of the Snows in the south of France. At his request, he was transferred to the monastery at Akbès, in Syria, because the poverty there was so great. But in the end it was not poor enough nor hard enough. He sought something poorer and harder still.

With the consent of the superiors, after seven years of Trappist life, he left the monastery and went to live in Palestine, at Nazareth, as the handyman for a convent of Poor Clares. Three years were spent thus; his only salary was a little food and shelter—a hut in the garden. He had found, he thought, what he wanted—solitude, to be unknown; he had taken, he hoped, the bottom place. But his solitary contemplations were interrupted by the thought of others poorer than he, the most forgotten people of all, who had no priest to care for them, no one to show them the gospel. His thoughts continually returned to the Sahara.

He went back, therefore, to our Lady of the Snows, and prepared for ordination. At the age of forty-two he received the priesthood and set out to work among the Mohammedans of the Sahara. He would bring Christ to them, not by preaching —they were not ready for that yet—but by the example of his daily life.

He dressed in a white habit with a rough red heart of serge sewn upon his breast, the badge of his apostolate. Fr. Charles of Jesus he was called now. He went first to the oasis of Beni-Abbès, living there a life of incredible hardship, sleeping little, eating only the simplest food, and that in small quantity. Daily he prayed for others to come and share his work; he saw the desert peopled with little hermitages, whence the Christian message should radiate by the example of a holy, self-denying life. But no one ever came, and he remained alone; his dearest wish was granted though, he was unknown and forgotten.

The natives—the Tuareg Arabs—were quick to appreciate him at his true worth. They trusted him and called on him for help in all their troubles. Soon his medical stores were exhausted and he had to send home for more. For hermit as he was he was eager to receive anyone to whom he could do good.

In 1906 he moved from Beni-Abbès to Tamanrasset, right in the heart of the Sahara, in the Hoggar, a thousand miles from Algiers. From now onwards until 1914 he divided his time between the two places. Down in the Hoggar, as in his first post, he soon became beloved of the Tuareg tribes. The secret of his success was his love for these abandoned people, the apostolate of charity that he practised, showing in his life the love of God for man, carrying out the maxim that was his devise: 'To proclaim the gospel by my life.'

He was the 'universal brother'. He taught the Tuaregs to cultivate vegetables, and endeavoured, successful in part, to make them give up their nomad bandit lives. He initiated the women into the mysteries of knitting and chocolate making. The direct preaching of the gospel would not come yet. Twenty-five, fifty, a hundred years later perhaps these peoples might be ready for it. For the time all he could do was to teach them the natural law. His was the preparatory digging of the ground; those who came afterwards might begin to plant, to cultivate.

There at Tamanrasset he met his death on a December evening of 1916, and that, when his life was first written, was the end of the story. His example, his prayers, were bound in the end to have their effect; men sought to do as he had done, to carry on his work.

Recent events in Algeria have made Fr. Charles de Foucauld into almost more of a period piece than he was before—or so it would seem. But in considering the man and his work we have, as always in considering those who lived at a period different from our own, to abstract from the purely circumstantial elements of the story in order to concentrate on what is of lasting value. We must therefore examine de Foucauld's method a little more closely in order to obtain an idea of his significance at the present time.

When he was in Beni-Abbès he drew up a carefully arranged timetable which he endeavoured to follow there and in his other hermitage in the Sahara. It was to be a life of solitude and contemplation. But it had another side. For he regarded his mission as that of being the 'universal brother', to preach, through living it, the charity of Christ. So he was at the beck and call of all and any who came to him for help. There were the soldiers of the garrison, far from their native France, who found in him a true comforter in their difficulties. And the lower their rank, the less important they were militarily, socially, with the greater deference and consideration did he treat them.

Nor were the French soldiers his only callers. Little by little his cloistered, lonely life suffered a veritable invasion. The poor, orphans, slaves soon found him. He was unwilling to leave his enclosure, yet, metaphorically at least, he went out to meet them. He distributed barley on Saturdays to the needy, and got ready a room for guests. He ransomed slaves—in one year, 1902, as many as five—care of whom, for a time at least, fell upon him, and the hospitality of his hermitage. He began teaching them the catechism, and one, a child of three, Abdjesus, he baptised. As there was no one else to look after little Abdjesus, he fell to Fr. Charles's care and took up a great deal of his time. His timetable, so carefully prepared and ruled by an old alarm clock, had many holes knocked in it. But it was all part of his plan.

In later years Fr. Charles defined very well the scope of his mission in the Sahara. He wrote a Directory for the association of prayer for the conversion of the heathen that he founded, and his words give so clear a picture of what he was out to do, that I quote them here:

Remembering that our Lord Jesus has said: 'When thou makest a dinner or a supper, call not thy friends, nor thy brethren, nor thy kinsmen, nor thy neighbours, who are rich, lest they also invite thee again, and a recompense be made to thee. But when thou makest a feast call the poor, the maimed, the lame, and the blind. And thou shalt be blessed, because they have not wherewith to make thee recompense: for recompense shall be made thee at the resurrection of the just,' we shall then direct our efforts towards the conversion of those who are spiritually the poorest, the most crippled, the most blind, the infidel peoples of missionary countries; those who know not the Good News; who have no tabernacle, nor sacrifice, nor priest; the most abandoned souls, those who are most sick, the sheep that are indeed lost.

But he harboured no illusions about the difficulty of the task before him. It was his constant conviction that with the poor sons of Islam it was hardly possible to start right away presenting them with the great Christian dogmas. They must be prepared by charity and prayer. This, to the best of his ability, he did. In another small book written in the solitude of the Sahara, and called *The Gospel shown to the Poor People of the Sahara*, he develops this point at length. He wrote also so that when the time came he, or more likely his successors, should be ready for the work there would be to do—the reaping and garnering of the great harvest that was waiting. He understood that future audience and their ways of thought; the apostolate must be adapted to them. When a voice, not his perhaps, should be uplifted in the desert, it must not cry in vain.

He knew with what he had to contend. How often had he heard the boast that is also the *Credo* of the Mohammedan.

His answer had no need of boasting, but it was clear and to the point: 'The last of the prophets was our Lord, Jesus, whom God promised to Adam . . . between Adam and Jesus were many prophets, the chief of whom were Noah, Abraham, Isaac . . . Malachias, John the Baptist. Since our Lord there have not been, there will not be any until the end of the world, for God has taught us by the mouth of our Lord . . . our religion will remain until the last judgement, without any change.' God is always God, but Mohammed is no longer his prophet. Although Fr. Charles wrote for the future, his mission was extremely clear to him: 'One must not try to make conversions for a long time, but to seek to love, to cherish, to enter into close contact with the natives . . . if this is done, at the end of a variable time . . . twenty-five, fifty, a hundred years, conversions will come of themselves in the same way that fruit ripens on the tree, and in proportion as the general education of the natives increases.' But he saw well that if the Mohammedans of the desert never saw a priest, never came in contact with Christians, save with men who were Christian in name alone and sought merely to exploit them, giving an example not of virtue but of vice, the way of their conversion would be blocked and they would come to hate our religion.

This then is the explanation of the upsetting of the time-table. 'The fraternity which is very quiet at night,' he writes, 'and from ten to three in the afternoon, is an absolute beehive from five until nine in the morning, and from four to six in the afternoon' (July 1902). A month later it is much the same story. 'From half past four in the morning until half past eight in the evening I don't stop talking and seeing people: slaves, the poor, the sick, soldiers, travellers, the curious. I celebrate Mass before day-break. In that way I am not too much disturbed by noise and can make my thanksgiving in quiet, yet however early I may be, I am always called away three or four times during my thanksgiving.'

Charity, then, was the keynote of his apostolate to the

14

Tuareg. It was the same with the laborious compilation of the Tuareg–French dictionary and grammar which he prepared as a tool for others to use in after years when he was gone. Yet to understand Fr. Charles's mission we must look deeper than these merely exterior manifestations. If we read his life aright, one thing stands out in startling clarity—his passionate, burning love of our Lord. From the time of his conversion when he discovered our Lord as a *person* and gave himself to him, his whole life became directed to that end—love of him; in his exterior activities as in his interior life we have to look no further than that. The whole purpose of his life was a loving imitation, so far as he could, of our Lord.

True friendship leads to the sharing of cares and joys, of the lot of one's friend. Fr. Charles's essential work, then, was to share in our Lord's work, and he did this by constant prayer, continual intercession for the salvation of all men and, more particularly, by sacrifice and a sharing (in his small measure) in the sufferings of Christ. His apparent failure, too, can be seen in this light, for to his contemporaries his death in silence and in solitude was a scandal, as was the death on the cross to the Jews.

In such a life of prayer, lived in voluntary poverty and the solitude of the desert, charity to his neighbour expressed through his constant intercession, might have sufficed. But his vocation had another side, and it can be seen in action when Fr. Charles left Nazareth to be ordained, when he left Beni-Abbès to penetrate to Tamanrasset, nearly one thousand miles from the coast. He built his hermitage near the village, he seems to seek contact, pays visits, tours the countryside seeking out those who do not come to him; he is always ready for callers—he is the friend who can be found ready and willing to help at any hour of the day or night.

Not only hospitality, care of the sick, and such works of charity expressed his love for the Tuareg but his dictionary and grammar of their language, his collection of their poems,

15

his careful noting of their traditions and their customs were all part of his love. All this no doubt can be seen as the indispensable preparatory work for their conversion—no doubt it was—but in Fr. Charles's mind it was much more than that: he wanted to be their brother, to share with them on a basis of friendship, of love, and so he sought to know them intimately, for knowledge is the root of friendship.

His vocation, then, was a vocation of *presence* among the Tuareg, to be among them and of them; a presence, and at the same time a witnessing to the charity of Christ. He sought to proclaim the gospel by his life, and his mission was accomplished not by what he did but by what he was. By showing love to the Tuareg he spread the charity of Christ. In his view it is the fact of presence that is important; to be there, to be easy of approach. It is obvious how very much to the point is all this in modern missionary work. A desert tribe, the most abandoned people he could find, was his particular field, but his method is of universal application.

The great missionary problem of our day, both at home and abroad, one that is far greater now than it was half a century ago when Charles de Foucauld was proclaiming the gospel by his life in the Sahara, is one of communication. In the modern technological society as, under different circumstances de Foucauld found in the Sahara, the difficulty is the insertion of the gospel message into a culture that is vastly different from that in which the gospel has been, so to say, acclimatised these many centuries past. And it is there that the message of de Foucauld's life is valuable and that this man of that vastly different pre-1914 world has something very important to say to us and offer us; not a cut-and-dried method, not a practical solution, but a way of life that in its broad outlines is applicable universally under all conditions and in all circumstances.

A way of life but not a slavish copying of all the details of de Foucauld's daily existence; it is the fundamental principles that are important, not the manifestations of his religious practice. Nor are his political or military ideas necessarily to be copied; it is clear that he was a supporter of a colonial policy, of a form of colonialism that has now been discredited. Even his death can be seen as a direct result of some of his political activities, for he seems to have acted as a French intelligence agent in the desert during the first two years of the war.

If they are interpreted universally, and not in the context of the desert where they were first applied, de Foucauld's principles of a form of religious life (in the technical sense of the term) can be seen as a new invention, something not elaborated before. It is true that St. Vincent de Paul told his first Sisters of Charity, 'Your monasteries shall be the houses of the poor, your cell shall be a rented room, your chapel the parish church, your enclosure obedience, your grill the fear of God, your veil holy modesty.' But de Foucauld's ideas go much further than that, as we shall see.

There were imitators soon after his death. In 1929 Fr. André Poissonier, O.F.M., went to Tazert in the Atlas Mountains and lived a solitary religious life among the Berbers; his direct inspiration was the example of Fr. Charles de Foucauld, whose life, by René Bazin, he had read at the time of leaving school. A year previously Fr. A. Peyriguère settled in El Kbab in the Atlas and gave up his whole life to the Berbers. He died in Morocco in 1959. Readers of Raïssa Maritain's *Adventures in Grace* will recall Fr. Charles Henrion. While still a layman he was director of Eve Lavallière, the converted French actress, who finished her life as a solitary in a village in the Vosges; he was later ordained priest by the archbishop of Carthage and, joined by Fr. Malcor, an ex-admiral, went to the Sahara to live a life not unlike that of Charles de Foucauld.

But these were sporadic individual attempts and, like de Foucauld's, came to an end with the death of those involved. There could be no thought of any continuity. Yet, only a few years after Fr. Peyriguère had settled at El Kbab, foundations of a different sort were made which fulfilled to a great extent the desires of Charles de Foucauld, and at the same time held hopes of not passing away with the death of the founders.

In the course of a few years, almost spontaneously and practically simultaneously, small groups came into being independently of each other, but all looking to Charles de Foucauld if not as their founder at least as their patriarch and model. In August 1933 were founded the Petites Sœurs du Sacré Cœur, followed in September by the Petits Frères de Jésus. In 1936 a further beginning was made; this time it was the Petites Sœurs de Jésus, whose definitive form emerged in 1939.

Here we are concerned with the Petits Frères de Jésus. After he had left the Cistercians, Fr. Charles de Foucauld drew up three successive rules for his followers, though in the event, as we have seen, none ever came to share his life. But these sketches of a rule, although in some respects they were very detailed, could hardly be put into practice just as they were written, so that the groups which were founded after his death could only look to his general inspiration and were obliged to devise their own rules during an experimental period which even now has hardly come to an end. This has been an inestimable advantage to them; in these days, when the older forms of religious life all stand in need of adaptation to modern conditions, the Petits Frères, in a rapidly changing world, have been obliged to write their rule in the light of their recent experience.

In Paris in 1932 five former students of the Saint-Sulpice seminary soon after their ordination were all imbued with a great admiration for de Foucauld—they had read Bazin's biography and the volume of spiritual writings collected after de Foucauld's death. They decided to follow in his footsteps and together, for mutual help and support, to found the Petits Frères. On 8 September 1933, at the Montmartre basilica, Cardinal Verdier clothed them in the religious habit, a copy of that worn by Fr. Charles. At once they set out for El Abiodh Sidi-Sheikh, not far south of Géryville at the gateway to the Sahara.

El Abiodh is an important place of pilgrimage containing the tomb of a celebrated marabout. These first Petits Frères found an abandoned building in Arab style. It was hardly a 'fraternity' in the de Foucauld sense, but resembled rather an oriental monastery. This first attempt obviously called for a certain amount of improvisation and was based on de Foucauld's Rule of 1899, when the idea of small communities of what could only be called near-Trappists living in native, non-Christian environments was uppermost in his mind. Thus at El Abiodh these first Petits Frères lived a monastic life, with choral office, long periods of silence, daily sung conventual Mass, and rising in the middle of the night for prayer. They endeavoured to lose their European *cachet* by learning Arabic and by the use of that language for their common prayers. They devoted a considerable portion of the day to manual labour, tilling their garden and seeing to the upkeep of the establishment, but they never succeeded in living solely from the work of their hands and depended to some extent on charitable gifts made to them. In addition, though they were living in a milieu not unlike that experienced for some years by Charles de Foucauld, they had not that intimate contact with it which he enjoyed. Their monastic rule cut them off from the local inhabitants, although their dispensary and care for the sick did, on occasions, bring them closer. They were living among the natives, but not with them as de Foucauld did.

Then the form taken by the poverty they practised, although it was in every respect in accordance with the prescriptions of canon law, could hardly be compared with that of those among whom they lived. The poverty of the natives was the genuine article. The Petits Frères were, in fact, feeling their way and, learning by experience. Gradually their numbers increased,

19

so that by the beginning of the war in 1939 they were fifteen all told.

In some ways the war was a blessing in disguise for them. If they had continued together at El Abiodh it is possible that their way of life would have grown into a fixed, static form of one period of their evolution and that they would have remained a monastic order, following de Foucauld indeed in some of his ideas at one stage of his development, but failing to apply the fundamental principles that underlaid all that he tried to do. But the war dispersed the Petits Frères into the army and other forms of war activity, so that they were thrown in at the deep end and found themselves at grips with a de-christianised society and with poverty of a kind they had not experienced before. It is fortunate that their study and meditation on de Foucauld's message at El Abiodh enabled them to apply it to their new surroundings and that they could see how universally applicable it was. A contemplative life lived in the desert holds out a kind of romantic attraction, and, more than most, perhaps, the French are addicted to a sort of desert *mystique* (in addition to de Foucauld and names mentioned above, one thinks at once of Ernest Psichari, Louis Massignon, and, at an earlier period, that strange figure René Caillé).

What the Petits Frères learned from the war was the fact, which emerged from de Foucauld's teaching, that the desert was a symbol—it was the *deserted* milieu; he had, it will be recalled, seen himself as a missionary to the most forgotten ('abandoned' is the word he uses), the poorest, the helpless—the under-privileged, as we should say nowadays—and such as these are not to be found exclusively in the Sahara or even in the Near East; there are many of them in Europe, North and South America, and the British Isles. But it was not only the milieu that was important, it was also the form of life that needed to be far less confined if de Foucauld's message was to be given its authentic interpretation. Reading of his life reveals the continual tension in it between two of its components. On the one hand, was his hermit life with its silence, long prayers, and solitude, and on the other, there was his constant desire to share the life of those among whom he lived. So he was drawn in two directions, and what emerged from his example was a further development of his teaching.

The Petits Frères, in following this example, brought his teaching to its logical conclusion by combining the two fundamental points: theirs was to be a contemplative life lived in the very heart of the dechristianised masses[1] anywhere in the world. Their desert might be the Sahara, but equally well it could be the populous working-class quarter of a large industrial city, a native village in India, a mining town in Belgium, or an oil refinery in the Persian Gulf.

Such a way of life required changes in the rule; there could be no question of monastic silence or large houses with monastic enclosure. The Petits Frères established small fraternities where communities of three or five could live as a family under the same conditions and sharing the lives of the poor and non-Christians.

Thus at the end of the war El Abiodh was kept as the central novice house, and from it successive foundations were made. But foundation is a high-sounding word which ill-accords with the facts of the case, for in the religious world a foundation generally means the building or buying of a house. The Petits Frères rent their dwellings—a farm cottage, a working-class flat—or else have a hut in the native village. They go out to work to earn their living, they welcome their neighbours to whom they offer hospitality, though strictly in accordance with their means and rule of life. Their life is centred on the daily Mass, their daily time of mental prayer, and their hour of eucharistic adoration. Their life is a combination, then, of two

[1] *Au Cœur des Masses* was the title of the first collection of letters, etc., by Fr. Voillaume addressed to the Petits Frères. It was published in English under the title *Seeds of the Desert* (London and Indiana, 1955).

elements, work and contemplation which are not in opposition to each other, but as a French writer on Charles de Foucauld has pointed out, 'two slopes of the same mountain'.[1]

Their lives, as their rule makes clear, are aimed at imitation of our Lord's laborious life and this is to be achieved by their leading 'in poverty a contemplative life of prayer and work in close contact with men'. 'Prayer and work,' says Michel Carrouges, 'are one, just as the love of Christ and love of the poor are one.'

And it is love of the poor, as Charles de Foucauld loved the Tuareg, that makes the poverty of the Petits Frères so outstanding in modern society. They share the lives of the poor by living with them under the same conditions, in real poverty as distinct from what is usually understood by canonical or religious poverty. Religious poverty as it is generally interpreted today entails the inability of the religious, the monk or friar, the nun or sister, to possess anything. Whatever they need is provided by the community, in many instances frugally enough, in others on a more lavish scale. The individual's poverty consists in not owning anything in the sense that he (or she) has no dominion over what is provided for his (or her) use. Communities, as such, may be considerable property owners, powerful corporations with large resources. Now poverty as it is experienced (as distinct from practised) outside the monastic enclosure is somewhat different in scope; it embraces a whole family, not just individual members of it, and although it consists in a lack of property (in this it is the same for the private individual as for the monk or nun) it includes also the consequences of such a lack, among which is to be numbered insecurity and dependence on others—and also dependence on a weekly wage packet or, in unemployment, on the allowance made by the state insurance system, if any. It is probably in this last respect that the contrast with religious

[1] Michel Carrouges, *Le Père de Foucauld et les fraternités aujourd'hui* (Paris, 1963) p. 190.

poverty, as it is interpreted in accordance with canon law, is particularly obvious. A solemn vow of poverty, provided the religious is not guilty of some heinous offence, nowadays amounts in practice to security for life. All this is not to say that canonical poverty is meaningless or has outgrown its usefulness, but the contrast between it and actual poverty has been shown in this way in order the clearer to show the ideal of poverty practised by the Petits Frères. They *share* the poverty of those among whom they live—lower-paid labourers, peasants in under-developed countries, casual agricultural workers, and the like. This 'witness to the poverty of Christ' (in de Foucauld's words) is the clearer because it is easily understood by those whose lives they share.

Fr. Voillaume, in one of the extracts in this book, shows clearly the relevance of poverty in the transmission of the 'good news'. 'The redemption,' he writes,

> operates in such a way that the great commandment of fraternal love is practicable only in the spirit of the Sermon on the Mount. Only our Lord could have really propounded the seven Beatitudes as good news. For this latter is based upon a twofold reality: on the one hand, there is the brute fact that among men poverty, suffering, weakness, and violence exist; and on the other, the declaration that all these things . . . will henceforth be transformed for men, through our Lord's death and resurrection, into the means of achieving redemption, of bringing God's reign and the establishment of peace.

So the Petits Frères are witnesses to poverty in the world and in the Church. They practise religious poverty on the model of poverty as it is to be found in the world in all its forms as they encounter it in the various parts of the world in which they go to live. Yet poverty for the Petits Frères is not merely one of the vows of the religious life, an essential tool in the quest for perfection. It is also, and this aspect is equally important, an act of witness to the charity of Christ. The Petit Frère cannot do anything very much to alleviate the poverty of those among whom he lives; the offer of a meal sometimes, of assistance in some manual task, of help in sickness, may be an immense benefit to the individual, but seen in the perspective of the poverty of the whole community it can hardly amount to more than a drop in the ocean. De Foucauld's two watchwords of 'spreading abroad the charity of Christ' and of proclaiming the gospel by his life were realised by him through his sharing of the lives of those among whom he lived (particularly at Tamanrasset). The Petit Frère does the same, and through the sharing of the poverty of his fellows not only bears witness to the charity of Christ but also takes the first and most important step to alleviation of the poverty around him.

These reflections provoked by consideration of de Foucauld's life and of the extracts from Fr. Voillaume's letters, do not of course deal with all the questions raised by the phenomenon of the existence of the Petits Frères in the Church today. But it will have emerged, I hope, that this special form of religious life is peculiarly adapted to the needs of the present period; at a time when all the religious orders and congregations, if they are to survive, must be concerned with adaptation to modern conditions, the example of the Petits Frères deserves special consideration.

The letters which follow, written between 1950 and 1960, were addressed by Fr. Voillaume, the prior general of the Petits Frères, to his subjects. Unlike a previous collection[1] which dealt systematically with all the aspects of the religious ideal of the fraternity, these letters are concerned more particularly with some of the more difficult aspects of the life of the brothers: the subjects mentioned represent certain fundamental points which, Fr. Voillaume felt, it was very necessary to deal with at length for the further training of the brothers. 'It is far easier,' he remarks, 'to live effectively a life of poverty

[1] Op. cit. p. 21.

and work than to reach the perfection of brotherly charity and contemplative prayer.'

It is obvious that so novel a form of religious life—a contemplative life lived in the midst of the world—has its own difficulties and dangers, its own risks, too, and that in the short thirty years or so during which it has been developed it should have evolved certain special needs. This must be borne in mind in reading the following extracts, but it would be wrong to emphasise unduly the element of risk and danger involved in the form of life here envisaged. Fr. Charles de Foucauld was well aware that the form of religious life which he had in mind necessarily contained its own peculiar pitfalls, and while guarding against them saw them, too, as a challenge to be faced courageously; 'fear', he said, 'is the signpost of duty'. Risk also held its message for him, and as his life showed he interpreted it in his usual vigorous language: 'absence of risk', he declared roundly, 'is a sure sign of mediocrity'. All through the present book, which is concerned with some of the more difficult matters in a modern spirituality of the desert, the whole feeling of mediocrity is absent; rather is there an excitement almost, and an attractiveness shining through these pages which reveals their message as something novel in its appeal to the modern Christian, yet simple with that simplicity which is as old, and as modern, as the gospel.

PART ONE

Letters to the Petits Frères

I

The Second Summons

In our work, as in any human undertaking, time conceals a menace. The ideal pursued, the effort to pursue it, becomes a little worn, and we are led to mingle mediocrity with holiness. Time and advancing years bring the temptation to compromise between the supernatural imperatives of the love of our Lord and those of our human maturity. As each year passes by, more of us reach the decisive moment in the spiritual life when we must make the final choice between Jesus and the world, between the heroism of love and mediocrity, between the cross and an easy existence, between holiness and merely decent religious conformity. Not only individuals but also the Brotherhoods themselves come to this maturity. Am I alone, as I contemplate the reality of our response to our Lord's summons to follow him throughout the world, when I sense this danger of insipidity and hopelessness in face of the immensity of the work he wants to achieve by means of the Petits Frères? I am speaking today to those brothers who have long been professed rather than to novices or to the newly professed, though these latter have everything to gain from a realistic and courageous insight into the demands which the religious life, in the not very distant future, will make upon them. To learn how to pass through the successive stages of Christ's growth in us with a generous heart is as important as the good beginning when, at our Lord's first summons that led us to the novitiate, we left all things in order to follow him. This perseverance is essential, for there is no point in starting if we give up before the end. Brother Charles of Jesus remained faithful all his life to the family motto which he cherished: 'When a task has been begun, there must be no leaving off until it is finished.' It is not enough to leave the boat and the fishing nets in order to follow Jesus for a spell; what must be done is to travel all the way to Calvary, and there to receive its message and its reward, and, with the assistance of the Holy Spirit, mount to the climax of a life completed in the perfect existence of divine love.

When we began we had as yet no experience of the natural and human *impossibility* of our living in harmony with the supernatural realm of the counsels. In youth a kind of correspondence exists between the generosity natural to that age and our Lord's summons to leave all and follow him. Poverty, chastity, obedience, prayer, and divine love—these do not then seem to present us with insurmountable difficulties. And also the divine pedagogy of the Master who summons us, itself assists, to some extent, in maintaining a temporary illusion, without which no one would have the courage to leave all things in order to follow Jesus and to carry his cross.

As time passes, however, and in accordance with the action of our Lord's grace, gradually, unconsciously, all this begins to change. Human enthusiasm gives way to a kind of insensibility with regard to supernatural realities; our Lord seems to become increasingly remote, and, on occasion, sheer weariness overwhelms us. The temptation to yield to our inclination to pray less or to pray by mere routine is more insistent. Chastity presents difficulties we had not foreseen. Altogether new temptations arise. We feel sluggish, and are more apt to seek sensual pleasure. Also, we tend instinctively and without being aware of it, or considering it to be wrong, to lead a rather more independent life, disregarding our superiors. Frankness seems less necessary; charity more difficult. The effort to adapt ourselves to other races or peoples sometimes leaves us discouraged; at the start everything seemed bright, but now we can only observe irritating defects. Criticism becomes normal; we fail to speak the language others use, or even to understand it. Poverty becomes a hardship. We hold tenaciously to our own ideas. Sometimes we wish for better food, and would like to feel more free. In general, we think—if only our lives could be more worthwhile! Throughout all this, no word from our Lord reaches us; he is silent; no longer does he give us the joy that we can *feel*, the joy that made it so easy for us to regard every prospect with optimism.

These experiences are quite normal, and they need imply no serious infidelity on our part, nor any abandonment by our Lord. Even if we keep fundamentally loyal to the demands of the religious life, we are bound to experience, to a greater or lesser degree, these various impulses or temptations.

In short, we are *progressively entering upon a new phase of our life*; we are finding out, to our cost, that the demands of the religious life are impossible.

If we fail to approach this stage frankly, fail to realise that it is radically impossible, with merely human means, to live a supernatural religious life and to help Christ with his cross, we incur the serious danger of either succumbing to paralysing discouragement, or deceiving ourselves by lowering our ideal to an acceptable level, a level that can be lived, or, in short, one that is possible. This, in fact, is what most often happens at this crucial stage of the religious life: *discouragement*, or *the half-conscious acceptance of mediocrity*, because in order to make the religious life livable we have in reality introduced an alien element. We have tried to find for ourselves some centre of human interest, some motive for living which, for good or ill, can be reconciled with the externals of religious life and with the decent observance of the generality of our commitments. But if, through clear-sightedness and a desire to remain truly faithful to our Lord, we reject such a compromise, then discouragement lies in wait.

And yet if only we could realise what Jesus expected from us at this critical moment of our religious life, if we knew what he expects from a stage which is not a step back, as we tend to think, but the establishment of the conditions necessary for a new venture, for the discovery of a life in the spirit and in faith, then we should also become convinced that, *with Jesus*, a life like this *is* possible.

Once we have set out on this new course, a new insight will show us new demands which the attempt to put our Lord's counsels into practice imposes. These we must endeavour to accomplish with renewed generosity, renewed because no longer sustained by any emotional stimulus.

In any case, if we intend to continue to make progress, we must give ourselves wholeheartedly to poverty, chastity, obedience, and prayer, aiming at a steady growth in love. Our will must be freshly surrendered; the effort we made at the start of our religious life must be renewed, for love is centred in the free will, our most personal possession, needing to be filled with the life conveyed to us through our Lord's manhood. But the disciplinary labour involved in this second beginning will surely affect the deeper and more essential zones of our spirit. It is difficult to compare it with our initial effort, because our needs, our desires, and our instinctive drives are now turned towards different objectives. Increased self-knowledge has also uncovered deeper and more radical obstacles. Thus the generous self-giving of a novice and that of a brother who has taken his final vows will not be expressed in the same way. We should not judge each other, but try to understand. It would not be wise for a novice to attempt to live like a brother of mature experience, or for one who is professed to attempt to return to the life of a novice. And this is as it should be, provided that each brother gives himself unreservedly, is on his guard against the illusions peculiar to his own spiritual age, and responds to the summons to total renunciation which Christ continually sends forth.

In my view it is also true that the gradual discovery of the various modes of life which Jesus intended the Brotherhoods to pursue in the world, is now complete. A period of time was necessary for all the implications of their ideal to become evident, and for the imperatives of their contemplative life to be more exactly defined. Many elements of this ideal have become clearer and more precise as the other forms of brotherhood, the secular institutes and the Petits Frères of the ministry of the gospel have come into existence. These brotherhoods required time to develop before the needs they were to meet, and the new problems produced, simply by their presence in difficult environments, could become manifest.

In this way the Brotherhood itself, *as a community*, has reached an important stage of its maturity, and we must all take a new look at the contemplative ideal which is essential if its imperatives are to be loyally fulfilled. It is my hope that the realisation of this development will not move any of you to yield to the temptation of choosing for yourselves a solitary and independent evangelical life, rather than accept the limitations of an organised human institution. The message of love and renunciation, of evangelical poverty and prayer can be transmitted to large numbers of people only through an institution emanating from the Church. Now it is precisely as such an institution that God has brought the Brotherhood into being, so that a life and a spirit according to the gospel may be spread abroad, and that through this institution, a greater number may have access to holiness. We are aware, of course, that such organic growth holds its own dangers: the working out of a rule, the costly dispersion of members, the establishment of a minimum of central administration, houses for training and study. But how can we dispense with all this, without forgoing something which has been thought out, imagined, and decided by Christ? Religious congregations that develop will always be subjected to the same criticism as that which is thrown at the Church on account of her organisation; and yet the Church, in spite of her human blemishes, has the shape which Christ divinely intended.

I beg our Lord that, with this in mind, each of us and the Brotherhood as a whole may be found faithful to the grace of the new birth according to the Spirit, which will be bestowed on us at the coming Easter.

Island of St. Gildas, 17 March 1957

My mind often dwells upon that constant and twofold imperative which our life imposes on us: we must detach ourselves from all things and yet give our lives to mankind. For that is what is involved. There is no way of avoiding these contradictory aspects of our religious consecration. We are indeed bound to detach ourselves from all things, to hold on to nothing, to absolutely nothing, just as if we were entering a Carthusian novitiate!

And then I think of the imperative which requires our presence among men, of our assuming responsibility for them before Christ, of our sharing those conditions of life which plunge us again up to the neck into all the tumult, all the concerns of the daily life of the laity most productive of a materialistic outlook. But this is the road we have to take, and in my view it is precisely through this effective self-giving to men that in our weakness, poor Petits Frères as we are, we learn to keep faithful. It is in this presence and through these demands that our utter detachment must be achieved. Of course, we need the desert, but not always. We are not monks or hermits, even though we must share their essential disposition of a radical detachment from all created being.

We are not hermits, and it is my personal belief that we cannot reach total generosity or sustain it, especially at the time of our Lord's second summons, if we have failed to give our lives to men for their salvation. We are, in fact, vowed to take other men's burdens upon our shoulders, with all the dullness, and sometimes even the crushing weight which that implies.

We lack the ability to lead a supposedly angelic and solitary life; all the more dangerous because we should certainly form a wholly inaccurate idea of the life of the angels and of the vision of the mystery of love which animates the life shared by the saints! We have within us a vital need to love, and the necessity also, if we would break through the strait-jacket of our ego, for effective self-giving, springing from a great love. The most authentic grace of contemplation does not run counter to these essential needs of our human life; it transforms them and purifies their manifestations, and, as regards ourselves, even serves, as an instrument, of that hold which those we love have upon us, those to whom we belong, with that binding service, that wrenching from self love which results from it. Grace, in order to lift us above ourselves, proceeds to utilise this need for love which, left to its natural bent, draws so many far away from God. But, in this case, the need becomes, in God's light and strength, an instrument of divine love. Thus the contemplation of the mystery of love in the reality of God and in our self-giving to mankind that allows us no repose, far from contradicting each other, meet in unison in the undivided love, the beating of Christ's heart. A Christian, made one in love, becomes in this way, with Jesus, a shepherd of men, leading them to living pastures.

As we carry out our Lord's directives, then those who live far from him, the working masses lured to materialism, and others also, nomads, miners, pigmies, sailors, will come to form the flock which he confides to us. Yes, this is the flock that will take hold of you and keep hold (for those of you

35

who have a position of responsibility or service in the fraternities it is your own brothers who may be considered to form your flock). All these men are to be sought out and loved; it is they who will help you towards complete renunciation, as the Toureg helped Father de Foucauld, and as all mankind in need of salvation provided our Lord, in his agony in the garden, with the absolute motive for persevering even to his death. When doubt assails you, when boredom and discouragement confront you, kneel down and ask yourself what you have done for the members of your flock, and what scrap of justification exists for your being an unworthy shepherd. You may even have to ask whether in fact you have a flock at all. Is it true that you have been entrusted with them, have you really been given the desire to belong to others, body and soul? And have you then adopted them as our Lord has adopted them, and in union with him, so that for their sake you are enabled to live and die?

The Railway Station, Dijon, 24 March 1957

2

Obedience to Our Calling

The truth is that we pass our days to some extent in unawareness of reality. We exist in an enclosure, crammed with the illusions of a life based on the senses and with memories limited to a not very distant past. But whether we will or no, we shall be compelled one day to confront the essential problem: either Christ loved in a way that leads to total renunciation, with all that that entails, or else an ideal in conformity with some human career which, however attractive, is necessarily transitory and limited; an ideal with an overwhelming appeal to the passions always slumbering within us, ready for every pleasure which modern life is constantly offering, provided we are not penniless or bound to some form of labour without leisure! A few there are who suffer the torment of a metaphysical experience of absolute Being and of the nothingness of human existence, but all of us are led, through the progress of faith, to an encounter with the loving imperatives of an infinite, incarnate, dead and risen God.

I have said that there is no need to be surprised when we meet with difficulties; they may even be greater now that our Lord may rightly expect to find us stronger. These difficulties spring from ourselves, from the world as it is constituted, and from the development of the critical spirit in man. But they also originate from Another. Do you think enough of the existence of one who has a desperate desire to destroy the Kingdom of God on earth? His activity is seldom evident, and personally we are not much inclined to dwell on it; if our belief in the existence and might of spirits who have rebelled against God became too explicit, we might not be able to avoid excessive fear of these mysterious and powerful beings.

It is, however, absolutely certain and as true as you are alive, that this adversary will attack the Brotherhood, and he will do so in proportion as it draws nearer to Christ and becomes a greater threat to the dominion of evil, egoism, and pride in the world. Obviously, so long as we remain solidly mediocre, controlled by self-love or intellectual pride, or so long as we remain merely respectably religious, I do not think he has any need to bother. But, if the Brotherhood, faithful to its calling, begins really to act as the leaven of which the gospel speaks, then be sure he will be on the spot, to paralyse, frustrate, destroy! So we must expect conflict, and difficulties are inevitable. Undoubtedly we can count on our Lord's power and that of his mother, both of whom have mastered evil; but you know very well that the mystery of our freedom and of the personal effort required from us, remains intact. We have now corporately reached a position from which the adversary cannot refrain from summoning all his power to stop us. To shift from an attitude of indifference or of idle oblivion and fall into a panic of fear would hardly help matters.

And yet, is it not strange that although we have been enlisted in our Lord's service for many years, these thoughts of discouragement and of turning back only seem to appear when difficulties arise? Hitherto, perhaps, some have not seen clearly how serious their commitment is. They have made their profession to serve our Lord, and that profession has been publicly received by his Church. It binds us to our Lord, and its nature, which is intrinsically perpetual, loses all meaning if with the first difficulty it is made problematical. Good heavens! how many married men put up with difficulties and inner conflicts, often graver than our own, without the question of breaking the marriage bond and contract ever crossing their minds, for they know that it is indissoluble! For what reasons should *we* be less faithful in keeping a contract that binds us directly to our Lord? It is, nevertheless, precisely here, in this perseverance with respect to all things and in face of all things, in this binding power of constraint and attachment, that the greatest source of our strength resides, the most effective counterpart to our weakness and inconstancy. The Church, who has decreed that some men and women should bind themselves by a perpetual obligation to carry out the gospel in their lives, is well aware of this. And it is this which constitutes perseverance.

Because matters are not going smoothly in your religious life you begin to consider what personal fulfilment you would secure in a home of your own, and all at once you seem to realise how much easier everything would be if you had the affection of a wife and the presence of children who would compel your steadfast attention. With this prospect in mind, which in the hour of temptation seems obvious, the contract binding you to our Lord looks empty, drab, too much of a burden, and without apparent result. Then you come to feel that you were made for marriage and for an active and wholly interesting life in the world. That, you think, should have been your proper course, and from that moment the religious life may begin to look like a flight from those responsibilities which form a man's duties in the world. It is, of course, quite possible that there is some truth in this, for those whom our Lord calls to follow him are men like other men! You say that you have discovered that you were made for marriage; but obviously this has been true in every age and all men, even the apostles, were made for marriage! The position has in no way changed, except that our Lord is asking us to give up

39

and renounce precisely this, and he warns us, once we have taken this first step, not to look back, doubtless because if we do we shall no longer have the strength to go forward.

In each house of the Brotherhood there must be a minimum of community obligations: a fixed time of getting up, duly supervised, then the recitation of the *Angelus*, the *Veni Creator*, and Lauds. It must be only a real impossibility, for reasons independent of our will, that allows this minimum of prayer in common to be habitually dispensed with. In the evening, adoration, Vespers (often the most difficult to arrange), Compline, the evening *Angelus*, the communal reading of the gospel followed by a brief review of the day just past, the prayer of self-abandonment to God, and retirement to bed at a time settled by obedience, are normally of obligation. All this forms the minimum structure of that religious life to which obedience itself demands our loyalty.

Should this structure be absent, do not be surprised when weariness and torpor gradually take possession of your soul, and perhaps even a distaste for the religious life. We might say the same thing with regard to the day spent each month in 'the desert', the periodic hour of adoration in the night, the weekly half-day of recollection, all the more necessary when life during the week has been exceptionally disturbed or burdensome. You must give an account of all this from time to time to your regional superior or to me, and if in spite of every effort you find yourself unable to keep up this minimum, at least as a general rule, then you should notify us.

When you are travelling or are not in one of the houses of the Brotherhood, do not forget that you are still bound to the same observances, to the best of your ability. The recitation of Lauds, Vespers, Compline (or their equivalent according to the different rites or regions) is incumbent upon the brethren, just as the breviary as a whole is of obligation for priests. Even when alone, do your best to remain faithful to the

Angelus, the *Veni Creator*, the reading of the gospel, and before you go to bed, a brief examination of the way you have spent your day, followed by the prayer of self-abandonment to God.

Rome, 1 December 1957

3

The Eucharist and the Priest in the Fraternities

The eucharist is the Body of Christ, and it is the purpose of providence that we should be utterly devoted to the eucharist in a special way. We shall be failing in our essential calling, we shall be losing the true form of our apostolic mission to the extent in which the eucharist is not the real centre of our lives, our foremost concern, the factor that sustains our prayer and faith, the source of our apostolate, and of every act of divine love emanating from us. The eucharist is at the centre of the Church as both the sign and the reality which gathers her wholly into love and fuses her into a single sacrifice. In the Brotherhood, the eucharist, the blessed sacrament, must be all this, and in addition involve a special attachment resulting from a religious calling that may be said to be bound up with this sacrament.

The demands made upon us by poverty, work, an austere life and friendship are indeed essential. But they are essential only inasmuch as they are works of divine love, and this they would cease to be if they were no longer subordinated to the eucharistic prayer, to the fulfilment of the real sacrifice of ourselves, body and soul, in perfect obedience to our Lord and in total co-operation with his suffering and death on the cross. The whole content of our way of life is made known to us and communicated in the eucharist. We must, of course, be loyal to our ideal of incorporation in the masses of mankind, and of sharing the conditions of life of the poor. This outward loyalty, this presence here and now, is often the only aspect of our ideal accessible to those who appreciate us and sometimes means a constant and harassing activity in the service of others. But however great this loyalty and the praise it may arouse—for this, and not prayer, is what chiefly appears to men to be heroic and true—we shall no longer be anything, and our life will be emptied of its essential content if we are not loyal to the eucharist with the integrity of a faith wholly motivated by love.

We have the blessed sacrament in our midst, in our chapel, and our lives are spent in daily intimacy with it. To Father de Foucauld the blessed sacrament meant that our Lord was in the midst of the Brotherhood, sharing the life of the brethren and transforming their dwelling into an authentic home of Nazareth in which his Petits Frères were to live with him. How are we to understand this assertion and how far is it true? I have said that we must follow the instinct of love, but that instinct must be regulated by faith and it is right therefore to ponder over its content.

The blessed sacrament is a profoundly great and mysterious reality; nevertheless, faith teaches us the meaning of the eucharist in its essential simplicity. It includes two main aspects: the reality signified which is the actual presence of our Lord's glorified manhood, and the creative sign of the bread and wine and of the sacrifice, which transmits life to us and thus progressively transforms us into God. This two-fold aspect of the sacred eucharistic reality turns us both towards our Lord and towards his mystical body, towards God and towards our brothers whom we are to love. During the years that remain to us, our chief effort must be to try to conform our inner attitude and our whole life to this two-fold reality. To act towards the eucharist as we should to-wards our Lord's manhood is the expression of an attitude that is objectively true, and one that it is a special duty for the Petits Frères to cultivate. But it is not enough; we must also allow ourselves to be transformed and changed by the eucharist as a sacrament to be received, and we must co-operate with all our might with that self-conquest at which the grace of the sacrament aims. These two realities are simple, and on our part they entail a total self-giving to our Lord and to our brethren.

For us, as for the generations before us, the sign of the eucharist is that of the calm and unchanging appearance of the bread and wine. But the reality to which this spiritual nourishment and this mystical offering are due, sprang from the anguish of a human heart, a sweat-drenched face, a body shuddering as it was racked by pain, wounds from which the blood dripped and the long drawn-out agony of a criminal's death. All this was borne for us by God. Without this torment of the Passion there would be no sacrament. The eucharist may be described as the link that unites each of us and all our days, with their store of small misfortunes and slight sufferings, to that which took place during those hours of our Lord's suffering as a man: the eucharist must be like a channel which, down the lines of the bygone generations and, as it were, outside time, communicates to us the suffering of the Son of man (according to our aptitude, of course, and yet most truly), so that we may have our part in it. If participation in the eucharist fails to move us to welcome all suffering as our share in that which counted most for Jesus, and still more, to seek out sacrifice, then our participation in it is barren.

There can be no eucharist without a priest, and no eucharistic worship without a priest's ministry, and that is why the Brotherhood cannot carry out its mission perfectly unless some of its members are priests.

44

It is not simply because experience has shown that when the houses of the Brotherhood did not include priests, the brethren found it more difficult to maintain the fervour of their eucharistic prayer, but, fundamentally, because it is essential to the calling of the Brotherhood to be thus dedicated to the eucharist. If we believe that our way of life has been providentially indicated by God, through the life, the devotion and the ideal life of Brother Charles of Jesus, we must not forget how and why he felt so strongly moved to ask for the priesthood, without which he did not consider that he could establish the Brotherhood. Even if all the houses of the Brotherhood had a secular priest from outside to serve them, so that Mass, the exposition of the blessed sacrament, and the nightly adoration might be faithfully observed, an aspect essential to the perfect expression of the calling of a Petit Frère, and for their mission in the Church would still be lacking.

Although the priesthood is necessary if the Brotherhood is to carry out its mission perfectly, we should not, however, conclude that no individual Petit Frère can carry out his mission perfectly unless he is a priest. The presence of Petits Frères who are not priests is absolutely necessary to the calling of the Brotherhood.

Those who experience the legitimate attraction of eucharistic worship may perhaps incur the risk of being drawn away from a life of poverty close to mankind, whereas those who follow that way of life more literally may perhaps incur the risk of ceasing to be faithful servants of our Lord in his eucharist. The loyalty of all our members to their common ideal depends upon the attainment of an equilibrium between these two tendencies in the Brotherhood, and hence it is normal for the brothers to experience something like a summons from God to give themselves more particularly to one or other of these two elements within one and the same calling.

45

The inward and essential reality—that which is perceived by our Lord—is common to all the Petits Frères, whether priests or not, and whatever the nature of their external commitments; this is the love of our Lord leading to a total imitation of him, and to the desire of sharing the Saviour's redemptive calling, through adoration, self-sacrifice, and the love of the utterly poor. The differences that mark the calling of each Petit Frère are, after all, wholly secondary to this essential reality; for these are concerned with the way in which the apostolic calling and eucharistic worship are carried out, with the service of others and of the Brotherhood. Whether a brother is called to the priestly ministry or not, whether he is dedicated to a particular body of men, submerged with them in some sordid toil, or assigned to serve his brethren in the discipline of their intellectual formation or in assisting them materially, is all of secondary significance in comparison with his essential religious calling; it must be envisaged in the context of the mission of the Brotherhood as a whole, within the Church. Having said this, we must now answer more searching questions about the special calling of a Petit Frère who is a priest.

In the first place we need a clearer idea of the relationship between the priestly calling of a Petit Frère and the general mission of a priest in the Church.

This calling of a Petit Frère to be a priest involves its own peculiar difficulties. The reason which made Brother Charles of Jesus hesitate when he was thinking about ordination to the priesthood is today as valid as ever; it is the difficulty of reconciling the status of a cleric, and the signs of a dignified position which the Church attaches to it, with the social status of poverty and toil essential to the calling of a Petit Frère.

Henceforward, this point must be completely clarified. For the difficulty that may possibly arise from the requirements of the clerical state must not only not be an obstacle to some Petits Frères becoming priests; it might even present itself as a motive in favour of such a calling. When Brother Charles accepted the priesthood he did not in any way give up the demands of his calling 'to the lowest place', he realised that he should unite them both. The Church certainly has no intention of identifying the dignity of the priesthood with any merely human dignity, even though such an identification seems sometimes to have been made spontaneously by the Christian people. The reverence often shown by the laity to their priests is not a matter of reproach. For inasmuch as external signs of respect are due to divine and sacred things, especially to the blessed sacrament, they are also due, in the same degree, to the sacerdotal quality of a priest and to his function in the liturgy.

Is it not also true that anyone who becomes a member of a religious order becomes, in the eyes of the Church, a sacred person by virtue of his profession?

Ordination dedicates a man to the service of the sacrament for the sake of the ministry, and religious profession dedicates a man to the service of divine love for the sake of a complete personal rebirth in Christ. From one point of view the act of making a religious profession is even greater, because its effect on the soul of the man who makes it is more profoundly redemptive. In fact, there has been an unbroken tradition in the Church which endows it with an exceptional power of purifying and rectifying the soul, comparable to that of baptism.

The point of these remarks is to show that the position of dignity attributed to the clergy or to members of religious orders is not intrinsically a question of position in society, even though in many countries circumstances have made it so. But, in my view, no great difference between the clerical or religious state is produced by this fact. Priests, monks, and nuns are usually thought of as belonging to the same social rank. It is not, therefore, essentially, so much more difficult for a priest-brother than for a lay-brother to strive to keep to the lowest place and to remain the brother of the most disinherited of mankind. Custom and some ecclesiastical regulations may, however, be a temporary obstacle to the achievement of the ideal of a Petit Frère.

When a Petit Frère has in fact been ordained, has he the right to refrain from performing all the various kinds of service which the laity may lawfully expect from a priest? By accepting the priesthood has he not put himself into a position which will inevitably lead him to answer—because divine love commands that he should—every request for his services to which a priest is subject: the celebration of parochial Mass, hearing of confessions, giving retreats? Are not the powers received in ordination for the service of the Church a source of obligation intrinsically superior to the observance of a religious rule? What reason can justify abstention when needs are urgent, abounding, and on the doorstep? Some of you have felt this problem deeply. The Petits Frères, true to their calling, are of course ready to meet the genuine imperatives of charity, as indeed their Constitutions direct. But to consider every request made by the clergy or the laity as an obligation would be a misunderstanding of some of the deeper imperatives of the special apostolate entrusted to them. This would also mean that the fact that the priesthood of individual priests is completely subject to the jurisdiction of the Church and the bishop had been forgotten. It is for the Church and the bishop, and for them alone, to decide on the way in which an individual priest must exercise his authority. He has no other obligation than that of being a perfect collaborator with the Church. But, as I observed above, through the approval of the Brotherhood's form of religious life, through the decisions of their superiors to whom jurisdiction has been committed, and through the authority of those bishops who have a house of the Brotherhood established in their diocese, the Church has in fact decided on the way in which she intends a Petit Frère to exercise his priesthood.

Brother Charles of Jesus had hesitated about becoming a priest because he had thought that, once he was ordained, he might no longer be able to avoid what was expected from a certain social position, whereas he felt that he had received an overriding call to embrace the state of poverty even in its utmost consequences of social degradation. This is an abiding and essential imperative for the Brotherhood. We must realise that it truly has a mission of witness within the Church and that its aim is to create a religious congregation that really belongs to the milieu of the poor and of lowly workers. We know what unceasing effort must be made, especially in some countries, if the Brotherhood is to remain, in absolute truth, a part of a milieu like that. The way in which the Petits Frères must lodge, be clothed, live, and work, is controlled by this purpose.

It is permissible to think that the providential mission of the Brotherhood also extends to the ecclesiastical sphere of the clergy. It cannot be possible for the dignity of a priest to be incompatible with the position of a poor man, and the special difficulties encountered by a Petit Frère who is a priest, in his effort to remain faithful to this position of poverty, must not deter those brothers who are called to the priesthood from receiving it. One aspect of their mission is precisely this: to reawaken in the clergy an awareness of this problem through the example of their lives. For the Church could not be fully missionary if the clergy as a whole remained exclusively bound up with a privileged social class. If we may speak of the witness to poverty, prayer, and friendship which a brotherhood loyal to its vocation is called upon to render, it is equally true to speak of the witness given *to the clergy* by a Petit Frère priest who remains faithful to the conditions of life of the poor and to their environment. It is especially true of some countries that the witness of the Brotherhood will be manifestly incomplete so long as the Petit Frère priests do not share the life of the poor and their social situation. The fact that a Petit Frère comes to be ordained in the place where he began to work in poverty and that afterwards he continues to live in the same circumstances, enables the wholly spiritual and supernatural nature of the powers received at ordination to be better understood.

Münster, on the feast of the Body of Christ, 5 June 1958

4

Friendship Among the Brethren

Should the divine and supernatural friendship which unites us with each other and with Christ in the sharing of a common life, a common love, and a common summons, be expressed in any other way than on the purely spiritual level of prayer and through sharing a common ideal? Have we not renounced the tenderness of human friendship? In short, should that friendship which unites us to each other in Christ be given human features and have a natural basis for its foundation?

You know, of course, that the love poured into our hearts by our Lord must be a love of mutual good will, just as it must be established between persons who are in communion through sharing the same reality. I have often talked to you about this.

But in that case how do we account for the fact that among ourselves, as very often among priests and members of religious orders, this friendship remains submerged in the inner man, entirely 'supernatural', of course, but incapable of being expressed in joy, mutual collaboration, the intimacy of a true fraternal life? How do we account for the fact that this divine friendship that has brought us together fails to acquire human features and find expression in a visible friendship, a sign of the splendour of the divine friendship which unites us all? It is when we are *seen* to live in a tangible friendship, visible and human in its expression, that we shall be recognised as our Lord's disciples.

We did not freely choose each other, but it is the same

summons from our Lord that has gathered us together, and now all of us have been called by the same love in order that we may achieve the greatest and deepest of all possible friendships. It is a fact that we have been gathered together in this way, and yet, on the natural level, we are still not mutual friends. It is our Lord's friendship that has gathered us together, and the human features of friendship, visible in ourselves, is something we must labour to produce. It is our duty gradually to become true friends, even though it may seem that by nature we are not self-evidently made for each other. This, then, was the problem to be solved. And it is precisely about these human features which we must give to our friendship that I am going to speak to you today. It will be like the body which you will bestow upon your supernatural friendship to bring it to perfection. I am convinced that if you do this, you will be meeting the demands made by the friendship that unites you to our Lord even more completely.

It is true that the love of friendship which unites us to our Lord also demands that we should love all our brethren in like manner. But this seems obviously impossible, unless indeed we are talking about something other than genuine friendship.

The restrictions imposed by human life on earth make it impossible for us to acquire and exhibit feelings of friendship towards any considerable number of our brethren, and, *a fortiori*, towards all those who cross our path. How, then, can it be possible for the love of friendship in our Lord's name and expressed towards all men to become the perfect fulfilment of the commandment to love? In fact, however, Jesus does not ask us to acquire a conscious feeling of friendship towards everybody, but to have a heart sufficiently open and humble and alert to others, and above all spontaneous enough to be capable of friendship should it become possible here and now. We must understand the commandment to love, and try to obey it in terms of what is possible in our human situation as it actually is, a situation so confined that in reality we are able to have a few friends only. Why should this surprise us? Was not our Lord himself so restricted by his circumstances on earth that he was unable to have more than a very few men and women as his intimate friends? I am, of course, only talking about the feelings he experienced as a man; as God, his heart was even then overflowing with an infinite and worldwide friendship for all mankind redeemed by him. But, during his life on earth, only very few were able to know and experience his strong and tender friendship. Jesus was a man like us, and subject to the same limitations. But after his resurrection the power of his glory enabled his manhood to enter into a wonderful friendship with each of us. We also will come to share this quality. As our heart is trained and developed by his grace and love it will become a friendly heart even though it may in fact be able to achieve a real friendship with a few only. A hermit, for instance, could be transformed in this way by our Lord's tenderness and love, although he may not be given the chance to practise this friendship with any of his fellows. At the resurrection a heart developed in this way will have gained the capacity to welcome all men as friends!

When we learn to make friends we are imitating our Lord. It presupposes that our hearts become sufficiently detached from all things, sufficiently humble and generous to have the ability to create friendship. This, then, is the way in which we must interpret our Lord's commandment to love each other with a love of friendship.

Friendship is something so great and splendid that it is probably indispensable for human perfection. I find it hard to believe that a man without friends can be perfect; at any rate, I am sure he will be profoundly unhappy. Without a friend a man is imprisoned within himself.

As a rule we raise few questions about the nature of friendship or about what needs to be done if we would have friends, because we consider that friendship is not made to order, but is something entirely spontaneous. Does it follow that a friendship originates through the chance encounter of two beings born to understand each other, to have all things in common and to become friends? To some, spontaneity seems so bound up with the idea of friendship that without this absolutely free choice it would be inconceivable. Is there a hope of becoming a real friend of a man whom at first we regarded only with indifference? And supposing it is not just indifference but antipathy that we feel towards him? Or what if it is a question of a natural difference in taste and inclination, making companionship unthinkable except as something to be endured, demanding from us a constant effort to control our feeling and the maintenance of an attitude of 'supernatural charity' towards him? It seems to be a fact that when we think of friendship it appears to us primarily as a spontaneous achievement, an instinctive choice. Born to be friends, or not.

Friendship cannot exist without something to share, and this something must be good not evil. In friendship, giving and receiving are simultaneous. Everything that is good and noble may be its starting-point. In the case of the Petits Frères is not its basis that mutual assistance they owe to each other, not only in order that they may keep loyal to their external obligations but also, at a deeper level, that their love of our Lord may increase and develop? And yet a friendship of this kind may appear so fleshless, austere and lacking in spontaneity that we are unable to think of it as real. Friendship between two men, even if they are members of a religious order, seems to us to require a natural and truly human basis. And it is true that mutual assistance in loyalty to our Lord seems so difficult and remote from ordinary human relationship that we do not always visualise how this must be expressed in practice!

We feel strongly that friendship at any rate entails something different from a periodical effort to scrutinise life courageously and to renew it! There is no opposition between a 'supernatural' and a 'natural' friendship, as though in order to be supernatural it ought not to have a natural basis. If friendship presupposes an exchange between two brothers, how can an exchange consisting solely of supernatural realities be imagined? Is this not a really vague idea when we are concerned with a friendship between two beings of flesh and blood? No; natural must not be opposed to supernatural friendship. All friendship is supernatural as soon as it comes to exist between two Christians both equally anxious to remain faithful to all the demands of the love of God and of their brethren. Friendship is like life; it is no more possible for a purely supernatural friendship to exist than for supernatural acts to exist which are not first of all human acts. Do not be afraid of giving friendship a natural human basis. As long as we are on earth our activities are human, and, in friendship, we must share feelings, interests, joys, and sorrows that will always be human.

How could we fail to achieve friendship among ourselves? We are neither cloistered monks nor hermits, and we have to lead a life in common, not only a life of prayer but also the homely life of Nazareth filled with human contacts. There is a sound and natural basis for friendship between the brothers. The Brotherhood must have the genuine features of a 'brotherhood', and the brethren will not have these if each follows his own direction. As I have very often repeated, it is *together* that you must *think out* and *carry out*, day after day, the daily activities of your life in the Brotherhood. There are many things to be shared among brethren who not only have the same religious calling but also are dedicated to the same people, to the same tribe, the same neighbourhood, the same workers; who feel the need to know the men with whom they pass their time and to share their joys and sorrows; who experience the same desire to make their brotherhood welcoming, joyful, and their chapel alive with their prayer in common. There are plenty of things to be thought out together, learnt together, done together. It may be, indeed, that a more directly apostolic and organised life draws those engaged in it to a closer and more constant collaboration: a daily routine of manual work and friendship like yours, does not in itself demand so much. Collaboration can be avoided almost unconsciously, and each can follow his own direction without encountering that of his brother. And yet in every brotherhood there is ample material for an exchange of interests and for an increasingly intimate collaboration that will develop into friendship.

No friendship exists unless the need is felt to share anxieties, sorrows, joys, fears, ideas, tasks, projects, with one's friend. At the start this demands an effort of self-discipline. The path to friendship consists of *learning to share*, learning to give, and learning to receive. It is very important to become able to receive; for how else could our brother be encouraged to give, to surrender some part of himself? Sharing must come to be loved simply for the sake of sharing and not only because of its utility.

Friendship is not only a state of being open-hearted with one's brethren, it is (as we have seen) a mode of sharing and absolutely presupposes a response. It demands *reciprocal trust* and frankness. The gift of ourselves which we offer must be received with an attentive and respectful heart and calls for a return. Friendship is a welcoming encounter between two brothers. It can happen that a single brother who, for one reason or another will not accept this sharing, is sufficient to banish all possibility of a friendly atmosphere in a Brotherhood. How could there be any friendship if what we confide is received only by a distracted ear or draws down on us an unqualified rebuke?

Some brothers experience a kind of shyness in speaking about their relationship with God, their inner life, or their personal difficulties. . . . I ask myself whether any real good is served by keeping a part of ourselves secret in this way. It is not the fact of expressing in a direct and simple way what we are thinking and feeling that intrinsically constitutes 'self-exposure'; that depends upon the motive that prompts us to do so. Obviously, some confidences will be made only to an intimate friend; our reason for speaking will often be only for the sake of the friendship, because if it is to be complete it entails a mutual right to know everything that may legitimately be confided. We should certainly create a very serious impediment if we jealously reserved some secret part of our life for ourselves alone rather than share it with a friend. This reserve which we call modesty is probably only the instinctive reflex defence mechanism of a remnant of egoism which will not capitulate. It is only too natural and explicable! If, however, what stops us is in truth only a legitimate feeling of modesty, because so far we have not acquired the ability to be frank, we only need to overcome it once or twice in order to realise how beneficial the extinction of this paralysing timidity is. It is a self-enclosure which may seem at times to be a praiseworthy reserve with regard to the secret of our personal life, but it may occasionally be only the unconscious accomplice of a temptation which will quietly consume us under the shelter of this concealment.

The purest human joy will reach us through friendship, and without joy we cannot live. Just as supernatural friendship cannot be contemplated without the reality of a normal human friendship, so also, I am convinced, we must begin again to learn to value simple joys. There are pleasures and there is joy. Pleasures may be renounced; moral health bestowed by joy may not. Giving up some human satisfactions must not also mean giving up joy.

We cannot live humanly as men without human joy. *Accepted sadness*, sadness that is welcomed, is always at least an imperfection; it is a reduction of the power of generosity and love, and it kills hope.

We may, of course, sometimes be overwhelmed by many causes of suffering and sadness, and the most grievous are those which hurt our loved ones and give us a sense of impotency. But we must learn to suffer without sadness, to share the suffering of others, while at the same time introducing an element of human joy into it. God does not want us to be overcome by sadness. I do not think that it is ever laudable to give up any sound and true joy without good reason, and in fact we need to renew ourselves so that we may be enabled to reach the sources of some joys once more. I repeat, do not confuse sensual pleasure, the satisfaction of a passing whim, with joy, true joy. In every moment of our lives some joy lies hidden: we can pluck it if we are on the watch to discover it.

Strength, peace, and joy are to be found in the alert and appreciative welcome we afford to each definite slice of life which comes before us in every moment of time. We are too weak to embrace more than this tiny moment of the present. Our spiritual strength has been measured out by God to the scale of only one moment at a time. We cannot escape from the time process and that is a succession of brief present moments, in accord with our stature as men. If we are to concentrate our poor human faculties lovingly upon the present moment, we must, with our Lord's help, be without fear, without excessive worry about the future, and without harbouring depressing memories of the past. All of this is a hindrance to our living in the sphere of true reality and in the reality of God.

For a long time I have increasingly felt great courage and peace as I allow myself to be carried along, moment after moment, by the very definite current of the divine will. All useless worry can thus be driven away and the burden, now made lighter, of whatever task the present moment may produce, can be accepted with peace. You will see therefore that pessimism, self-absorption, cowardice are often due to the fact that we give free entry to impressions, premonitions, imaginations that are wholly unrelated to the humbler, simpler, always bearable reality of the present moment. That moment is always limited and simple when taken in itself and separated from all others of the past and future. When we are praying our inner silence is seldom broken by the concerns of the present moment, but almost always by those of the future.

Lima, 19 May 1959

5

Worldwide Love

The assembly in Rome of all Father de Foucauld's disciples for the celebration of his centenary has made the unity and the diversity of the Brotherhood very evident. You have been able to observe it yourselves: the diversity of the brethren in origin, language, and nationality. This is a state of affairs that compels us to strive for unity, in the name of Christ's love at work in each of us. This unity is one of the Brotherhood's essential tasks. It is also a difficult and sometimes painful task, and yet nothing could be more vital, for without such union, love would be only an illusory and ineffective feeling. It is, moreover, a work bound up with the Church, because the Body of Christ gathers together men of every tongue, nation, and race, into the unity of a single visible and divine society. Through the speed of its geographical extension and the diversity in origin of its members, our Lord has made it amply clear that the Brotherhood itself is also meant to collaborate, in its lowly way, in the establishment of this unity among men.

Fraternal love presupposes mutual understanding, together with feelings of respect and esteem. We, however, are divided from each other by differences which too often become the cause of misunderstanding, irritation, clashes, impatience, and sometimes of aversion which keeps love at a distance. These differences are many: they spring from temperament, education, intellectual outlook, family, professional or social circumstances, and, lastly, from nationality itself. It is this latter which I want to talk to you about today together with the difference in language it involves, and which makes contacts difficult to establish.

Is it not like a summons to attain greater love when we find ourselves brought together in this way in one brotherhood, differing in nationality, language, and culture? It compels us to widen our hearts and broaden our outlook. But this enrichment, at once human and supernatural, will not be obtained without renunciation or without suffering.

What do we mean when we speak of the universality of the Church, which does not belong exclusively to any nation? What do we mean when we say that the Brotherhood must not be either French, or even European, but genuinely universal? Lastly, what do we mean when we impose an obligation upon a brother to give up his own country, language, and culture for the sake of a worldwide love, and for a mission from the Church, a mission to be carried out on the level of mankind as a unity, far beyond the divisions between races and nations?

I think that it is useful to have the nature of the problem clearly stated, because difficulties often arise from an incorrect idea of what is meant by this worldwide love. Some men, for example, are saddened by the thought that they are natives of one country only and regret that a single culture has left its indelible mark upon them. Such reflections would lead to the question as to whether the vocation of a Petit Frère does not impose upon him the obligation to deny the land of his birth and become a universal man dropping all ties with his earthly country and becoming henceforward a member of the universal Church alone?

Attempts have been made to do this, and when it proves impossible to deny either one's own being or the culture in which one has been as it were kneaded, discouragement follows, and a kind of self-annihilation, a risk of losing one's

61

identity. May a Petit Frère still cherish a preferential love for his own country? And there are other questions also, perhaps more difficult ones, arising simply from the fact that the Brotherhood originated in a single country: the spiritual teaching of the Petits Frères was therefore thought out and expressed in the language of one nation, and the earliest experiences of their corporate existence which helped to give the Brotherhood its characteristic features are bound to have been influenced by the social circumstances, the way of life and the mentality of that same country. Is this an evil? Could it have been avoided? To what extent can we and must we react against it? For those brothers who are natives of other lands find difficulties not only on account of the language but also because this new form of religious life, this evangelical message is handed to them enveloped in a mentality and ways of living which seem to them 'foreign' in so far as these appear to be entirely related to a single country and even perhaps marked by the defects of a national temperament. This situation begets much hidden suffering; it produces temptations to rebel against certain ways of doing things, on the ground that these are not truly 'universal'. It also provides opportunities for criticism, for setting up oneself as a judge, for choosing between what one considers to be acceptable as having universal significance, and what must be rejected as marked by an excessive national particularism. There is all this without mentioning the thousand daily tiffs that become weighty through repetition, due to the fact of living in a brotherhood and a country of which neither the language nor the culture has yet been mastered. At times this produces a feeling of being stifled, of a constant dwarfing of the most natural human powers of action, of impotency either to expand, or to express oneself freely with the certainty of being understood.

Can the causes of such disorder be avoided? Are they, in fact, bad?

Is it really an evil thing that men are so different in temperament, culture, language, and means of expression? Was this diversity, which has too often been the cause of divisions, of violent and fratricidal conflicts, merely allowed by God in order to reduce the risk of a collective enterprise undertaken by the human race drawn up in its pride against him? This is what the story of the confusion of tongues at the building of the Tower of Babel gives us to understand . . . [It suggests] that unity of language and a collective human enterprise ran the risk of creating a proud sense of power in man which had indefinite possibilities . . . It is impossible not to be reminded of what in fact is happening today precisely on account of the increasingly close unity which is being created among men by the universal language of the exact sciences and technology. In the Church men are gathered together on the humble mind that believes in God and of a humble heart that loves. This unity is independent of a collective human enterprise: it can exist without it and it can co-exist with it, in so far as intellectual pride, the natural consequence of the power of human enterprise, is neutralised by humility.

In any case, this diversity of civilisations is an historical fact, and it also looks to us like a possibility given to mankind as a whole to attain a greater wealth of expression: since every individual and every type of civilization is in fact limited, men need to complete each other through their differences, so that all civilisations taken together and all human knowledge, may vastly extend and correspond with the indefinite and never satisfied aspirations of the human mind. This diversity, therefore, really constitutes a fundamental aspect of the spiritual patrimony of mankind, and we are appalled at the idea that a materialist civilisation might reduce humanity to the 'standard' uniformity of a single system of thought and expression. It seems to us that this would be like killing the most essential spiritual aspirations which man possesses. Should we even hope that the human race may be bound together by the uniformity of the spirit of a common language? It would be presumptuous to answer such a question. What is certain is that this type of standardised, universal man, belonging to no country on earth, and possessing no culture in particular does not and could not exist without involving the destruction of his own greatness, a greatness founded on intellectual freedom. Moreover, at the present stage of mankind's evolution, a man without a country is, by that fact alone, an incomplete and dwarfed being. It is certainly not by any levelling down of this kind that the higher unity of the human race must be envisaged, and the Church asks us to strive to reassemble in love and intellectual communion that which sin and evil have scattered and set in opposition.

No man, therefore, can achieve complete fulfilment without belonging to a country and a civilisation, with all that this entails of knowledge acquired, of human and moral values slowly accumulated and transmitted along the generations. Every human being has been truly shaped and educated by his native land, even as regards his psychology and his physical type. This is the reason why every man must love his country with a filial heart, realising what he has received from it. But countries and civilisations are like schoolmasters; their goodness varies. All civilisations have been slowly developed by men living together in society; they are altogether human, and this means that they always transmit authentic elements of culture, but also errors to the extent in which they have been developed from a partially false idea of man's real destiny and of divine revelation. Only a civilisation based upon a completely accurate idea of man and of revealed religion can be thoroughly good. In this respect, therefore, there will be differences between human civilisations and countries: there is no equality. Some may be nearer to the truly human and Christian civilisation, others may be more remote from it; some may be rich in material and technical values, others, poorer in these values, may yet be richer in wisdom and authentic spiritual values. The various countries, through their civilisation, shape men in their own image and draw them together in such a way that they develop a need for each other; they have become fellow citizens. This is why exile is such a grievous sorrow for man, and often causes a profound and irremediable imbalance.

The love we owe to men also extends to these countries and civilisations and every man has an obligation to love the land which has given him the best elements of his character. But no country is an absolute; every man must learn to evaluate the civilisation of his country, by the criterion of God, so that he can reject whatever elements it may contain that are contrary to truth and to the divine law, and try, with the help of Christianity, to acquire the human and religious values which he cannot yet find in his cultural patrimony. Christian civilisations and the countries which have benefited from them, bear as a result a heavy responsibility before God and man. It is always a difficult and sometimes a heartbreaking task to integrate in oneself spiritual values that are alien to one's own civilisation. It is at this point that a work of mutual assistance and fraternal collaboration, based on the essential unity between faith and love, has come into being among Christians and from the heart of the Church. This is one of the highest tasks of love on the plane of the international apostolate, and of the unity between thought and action among Christians.

It is sad to observe that the love which should flow through the members of the Body of Christ has not yet succeeded, even in Christian lands and sometimes even among the clergy, monks and nuns, and missionaries, in completely overcoming racial prejudices, national bitterness, and occasionally violent feelings of resentment towards other countries. It is absolutely essential that an effective outburst of love should now rip out these prejudices and resentment from Christian hearts. There will be no progress in the Church, no preparation of human hearts for peace, if priests and members of religious orders continue all too easily to allow themselves to be affected by the mentality around them, and to adopt the feelings of embittered nationalism that inspire too many of their fellow citizens. It is grievous to hear words of contempt or antipathy towards certain races or classes of men coming from the mouths of those who are the ministers of Jesus or whose profession in the Church is explicitly that of love—it dumbfounds us!

And yet, are we not faced by the same problem within the Brotherhood? Silently, but through the full impact of the facts, our Lord is asking us to strive without ceasing to eliminate from our mutual relationships everything that might cause division and to develop feelings of a frank and abiding friendship in him. It is not our business to criticise defective love among priests, monks, and ordinary Christians of different races or nations, we should be grieved by it and become through our own mutual love a seed of peace and union. If we do not, we shall no longer have the right to bear the name of a Petit Frère de Jésus, nor call our houses Brotherhoods. Let us refrain from being shocked by the racial and nationalist reactions of others who perhaps have excuses that we have not got, while *we* have not made the attempt to create the conditions for a brotherhood of true friendship among ourselves.

We have, therefore, the duty to respect, esteem, and love other countries and the authentic values of their civilisations. But with our present ignorance of these countries and their cultural values, how will this be possible? In former times this ignorance was excusable, for contacts were rare and reserved to a few. It was, moreover, unfortunate that they were reserved to those whose profession was concerned with politics or commerce; they could hardly be disinterested. Today the great variety and speed of travel and of every kind of communication has increased the number of contacts without always leading to truer and more sympathetic understanding. Such meetings, in fact, have provided opportunities for feeling how 'foreign' we are, with the sense of isolation amid people who do not understand us, that this entails. This obstacle of an inability to understand is lasting, and it is difficult to overcome, for its removal would involve the learning of so many languages and the acquiring of so much information that the effort would be beyond the power of most men.

This obstacle exists within the Brotherhood, even though travel, the intimate contact between brothers of different nationalities and general goodwill are favourable elements. But what is to be done about it? One solution that is always possible is a great humility of heart: this involves a determination to take a favourable view of those whom we have a special difficulty in understanding, showing them a sensitive respect that avoids every expression of surprise, every witticism and misplaced comparisons with regard to ways of doing things that differ from our own. Above all, it is essential to develop a strong conviction of the equality of all the brothers, whatever their country or their race, and to act accordingly. We must treat each other with mutual respect, so that individuals are enabled to forget that they belong to a different race or country. But, on the other hand, attention and eagerness to oblige, if displayed too often, can become in the long run as trying as inattention or being firmly kept at a distance. This is because both attitudes are a constant reminder to their recipient that he is ill-adapted and in the position of a foreigner.

At the same time, when a brother is not yet at home with the language, the customs, and the mentality of a country, he must be helped to feel at ease. Life in common and fraternal co-operation are essential to the religious life of the Petits Frères de Jésus and to the loyal fulfilment of their obligations. And yet only too often we forget this duty of hospitality, and fail to realise how seriously a brother who does not understand the language spoken by the brotherhood may feel isolated, entirely cut off from common life, and utterly restricted to a life on his own. If a casual attempt should be made to speak more distinctly, to explain what the conversation is about, to maintain contact and really bring this brother into the Brotherhood's communal life, it is short-lived; it soon becomes tiresome, and the silent presence of the brother soon seems quite natural, or else it is wrongly assumed that by now he is well able to sort matters out. Only those who have lived isolated for a long time in a country whose conversation and customs were unintelligible can form an idea of the pain and confusion which a year in such a situation can produce. To put oneself in the position of other people demands an unending effort of attention, imagining what our own needs would be if we were situated like them. But, as I have said, it is an effort that must always be discreet, so that the person we are trying to put at ease is not bored or made to feel that he is for ever being singled out. It is a question of tactful love, and in practice the brothers who manage to maintain the right approach are few enough. Some unintentionally cause pain because they are insensitive in certain matters, they must be told of this, and their attitude should express more humility and discretion.

Difficulties and misunderstandings due to national differences among the brethren must at all costs be brought out into the open, patiently and without offence. National shyness or modesty that is an obstacle to complete frankness in this matter must somehow be overcome.

There need be no surprise if this issue is not put right from the start [when the brethren meet] for an examination of the way they are living. It is from the brothers in charge that the initiative must come: it is they who must promote a mutual give and take, and a general sense of ease among the brethren.

A special responsibility falls upon those who are in their own country, with regard to brothers who have only just arrived and as yet find everything strange. Language is not the only difficulty; some will have to endure for a long while, and perhaps for ever, a feeling of expatriation which is hard to overcome.

Our Lord's presence in the Brotherhood compels us to do our utmost to alter those elements in our attitudes and way of life (even when these are in themselves irreprehensible and blameless) that cause embarrassment to brothers of a different nationality. They cause pain to our brethren and this is reason enough.

Travel, of course, helps us to discover other cultural values, but it will never be easy to escape from our own identity and to bring our own reactions into harmony with those of a new environment. In any case, there is a limit to what we can do about it, for although we may be able to correct some attitudes that cause pain to others, it is impossible to change everything which has been substantially incorporated in our personality through the education, the mentality, and the history of our country.

No man can destroy his own personality, apart from the sinfulness and the root of sin it contains. And yet love demands that we should be continually trying to adapt ourselves to others, to other countries, and other mentalities. Whatever our native land, we must all make a generous effort to acquire a true mutual love, that soars above our differences and is based on all the things that bring us together and unite us in a common bond, a common faith and love, and the strength to look at our brethren with eyes that can perceive all that unites and disregard all that divides.

At first this unrelaxing effort may perhaps only result in a *modus vivendi*, a mutually patient toleration, but it will end by binding you together in a solid friendship, above and beyond your differences, which in fact may come to be welcomed as a new and complementary reality.

You must also help each other to adapt yourselves as fully

69

as possible to the country in which you are living; this adaptation is made easier when a thoughtful brother takes the trouble to explain, correct, and encourage you in the lengthy task of understanding a people whom you have begun to love. At the same time you must have no illusions, and not set yourselves an inaccessible goal; for even though you love a people with sincerity, even though you have mastered its language perfectly, and as it were made its temperament your own, you will still be in some way tied to your native land, and it is right that this should be so.

Our Lord demands that our love should be that of brothers united above and beyond our respective nationalities, cultures, and contrasting traditions. But he does not ask us to discard them. Charity, therefore, obliges us to love our country in all truth and humility, and to love all other countries with respect, completely abstaining from making comparisons between them and from any assumption of superiority of one over another; charity obliges us to try to understand the point of view of others, and should we fail to do so, then humbly to keep silent, conscious of our limitations, and refraining from judgement; it obliges us to make an enlightened and continuous effort to lessen temperamental features or defects which cause pain to others, and to accept criticism for these faults; to cherish no bitterness or resentment when unfair judgements are made against our country and to be willing to admit the fact when these are well-founded, though also ready to defend the truth and our country's reputation; to take every means of learning the language of the country as quickly as possible and be eager to speak it in the brotherhood; to accept courageously and even joyfully, as a way of creating that witness to unity which the Brotherhood must provide, the inevitable difficulties of a life in common with brothers of different nationalities and also the feeling of being uprooted caused by a lengthy stay in a country other than our own; to abstain strictly from any unpleasant or ironical reference to any country or race whatever; to avoid joking, even good-humouredly, about anything relating to this subject; and then, when all this has been done, we shall always need to learn to tolerate, respect, understand, trustfully help each other and never cease to hope that we may become true friends. This friendship is, as we have often said, one of the goals our Lord has set before us; it is well worth the acceptance of the sacrifices that are necessary to attain it.

The history of revelation and of the Church teaches us that God himself needs the diversity of cultures and hence of nations and languages, in order to give full expression to his eternal message to mankind on earth. Without the existence of different modes of expression, he could not have transmitted the wealth of divine truths in human language. Every human civilisation is in some way limited, and because of this they are not all equally qualified to express a religious message, especially when this has to be expressed not in words only, but in that concrete language which is uttered by the life of a prophet or a righteous man. In this respect, civilisations do not merely differ; they are unequal to the extent to which they are more or less fitted to express some truth of the spiritual order.

God, therefore, made a choice; he chose a people, educated it, shaped its mentality and its culture, separated it from other nations, and made use of its genius and its language in order to transmit revelation to the world. Not once, throughout the entire history of revelation, did he make use of so-called universal men. Every prophet, every messenger sent by God bears the profound imprint of his native soil and culture. His own Son was to have his own country in this world, his village, his family, his Galilean accent. God did, in fact, choose Palestine in preference to other countries to be the homeland of Jesus. This is not the result of chance, it is a fact; it was necessary for God to choose a birthplace for Jesus. From this point of view, Jesus is not a universal man, belonging to no country on earth: he is an Israelite.

In her origins and in every age of her development the Church is inevitably subject to this constant law. She came into existence in Palestine and acquired a settled structure on the shores of the Mediterranean; she spoke Greek at first, and then Latin; her liturgies bear the stamp of the Greek, Roman, Syrian, and Egyptian genius; her abiding centre is henceforward geographically bound up with the city of Rome, and her legislation has been influenced by Roman Law, just as her theological thought is expressed in the language of Greek philosophy. Now it is certain that she would not be human, not attuned to the human situation, nor comprehensible to mankind without thus taking root in the countries of the world. The choice is controlled by God and it is not a matter of indifference; it would be erroneous to want to disassociate the Church completely from the successive contributions made by human cultures of undoubted validity, and to begin afresh, in the name of an abstract universality, to build a Church entirely unconnected with existing civilisations, on the pretext that this would make her universal. This would amount to saying that up to now she has not been so, whereas, in fact, the sign of divine omnipotence is to be seen precisely in its power to build a universal Church with materials provided by human civilisations belonging to a particular period and country.

God chose the time, the place, and the civilisations which befitted the birth of the Son of Man on earth and the building of his Church. It was not a matter of indifference to God that Simon Peter was a fisherman; Augustine, an African Berber; John of the Cross and Ignatius of Loyola, Spaniards; Francis of Assisi, an Italian; Vincent de Paul, a French peasant; and Teresa of the Child Jesus, a young French provincial. This they had to be if they were to be equipped to express their providential message in the Church in the way which God had foreseen.

72

The Church must always be adapted to the human condition, because she is the Mother of men and by their side. Nor is she able to express herself through men without a native land. The Church is universal not through the denial of her part but through her ability, in every age, to renew her message of faith and love in all its fullness and truth in men who belong to each new civilisation to the extent to which it incorporates values that are authentically human and true. From this fact alone the Church's message is always new and renewed, it remains the same and yet is completely up to date.

This spiritual wealth of the Church is the product of the many cultures and human modes of expression which she has been able to make use of and harmonise through the power of her love, in order to elucidate the divine revealed truth of which she is the guarantor and sole depository. Within her being there is a constant collaboration between the unified activity of the Holy Spirit which ramifies through all created diversity and that of human beings in the manifold ways in which they are actually constituted. The living Church, unendingly seeking renewal, has an instinct for selecting and utilising, each in turn, the human values in every country that will most aptly serve to elucidate some particular aspect of her message. This is especially true when this elucidation is connected with a new form of holiness, charity, the apostolate, or the creation of a new religious order.

Every new foundation in the Church is stamped, therefore, with a twofold imprint. It is rooted in the country of its origin, and then, by virtue of the inner law of the mystical Body, it grows until it affects every member of that universal Body, disregarding frontiers and existing above them all. To take part in a work of this kind is more difficult than to reach an understanding in the sphere of individual relationships between persons of different nationalities, because this involves universalising a spiritual way of life and an institution which was initiated and worked out in one particular country. After all, a religious order must begin somewhere!

The Brotherhood began in the Sahara: its founder, Brother Charles of Jesus, was French by birth, culture, and education; his spiritual teaching was originally conceived and expressed in French; most of the first Petits Frères were French, and the style of life of the early brotherhoods naturally bore the imprint of the Sahara or of France. This is simply a fact, and if it had not been founded in the Sahara, it would have had to be founded in some other country and the problem would have been the same! When men become Christians, and when they become members of religious orders their better qualities remain intact: the Church is made for men and by men. When a man becomes holy his soul acquires a universal quality, but he does not cease to be a citizen of some country in this world, and, as I have said before, no one of us can become a complete man and therefore completely Christian and holy, without the support of a social, cultural, and national background.

The founders of religious orders are not exempted from this law. These men, particularly at the beginning of their work, express themselves through their own gifts and their own language. The language of authentic holiness is always universally understood, but the transition from the individual characteristics of the founder to the universality of his work or of his spiritual message is not achieved without difficulties, without intermediary stages, nor without the spirit of renunciation and the general collaboration of great numbers of men.

When we take for granted the universal and truly supranational character of the great orders, such as the Benedictines, Franciscans, Dominicans, and Jesuits, we forget what the intermediary stages must have been. Of course, the extension of these orders was facilitated by the unity of medieval European Christianity, and this partly explains the speed of their diffusion. In modern times, when national characteristics have become more emphatic and civilisations diversified by languages that have grown further and further apart, the growth of a religious order in the Church has been made more difficult, not only on account of the divergencies we have mentioned but also because of the speed which modern means of communication seem to impose upon the diffusion of every new human institution, a speed which perhaps does not allow sufficient time for the necessarily gradual assimilation of spiritual values by people whose circumstances vary considerably.

When this transmission is only concerned with abstract truths of a scientific nature there is no difficulty except that of accurate translation. But when it is a question of a value so intimately related to human life as an ideal of religious life, an ideal expressed in some definite mode of existence, in the practise of poverty, in work and prayer, in really sharing the circumstances of the poor, circumstances which vary with each country, when an ideal of this kind has to be transmitted to other nations whose characteristics are often very different from those of the land of its origin, it is hardly surprising that difficulties should arise! These difficulties must be honestly faced, and the effort necessary to overcome them accepted, with the conviction that it will be a providential contribution to the Church's life and apostolate.

We may well believe that God did not select Charles de Foucauld to be the founder of a new spiritual family without good reasons, and also that it was not without a purpose that he allowed it to originate in a definite country and at a definite time, and its first foundation to be erected in the Sahara, in the desert. Every institution emanating from the Church must be true to its origins and at the same time become adaptable and universal. For those who are called to take part in this task, great detachment, humility, and love of truth are essential!

Whoever we may be, therefore, if we have received our Lord's summons to become a Petit Frère, we must accept his decision to originate the Brotherhood with Frenchmen. Nothing we can do can alter that fact. We must not only accept this origin but rejoice in it. Unless we do that, we shall be unable to collaborate in our Lord's purpose of making the Brotherhood increasingly universal, with this origin as its starting-point.

It was doubtless necessary for reasons, many of which are beyond our ken, that the Brotherhoods should have first been conceived and brought into existence by Frenchmen. We are indeed obliged by the universal mission entrusted to us by the Church and by the imperatives of charity, to do our utmost to correct our defects and to expand our hearts and minds to the dimensions of the Church. But we shall still retain more or less the imprint of the land we sprang from and our mother tongue will still be French. It would be unjust if brothers sometimes reproached us for this, in a more or less open manner, because they have suffered from our lack of understanding and our limitations. For, to the extent in which God means the Brotherhood to extend to every country, and as an example of unity between brethren of the most diverse origins, there must be a transition from a foundation thought out in France to that of an assembly of brotherhoods distributed throughout the world.

There is, therefore, a twofold work to be done: that of the French brothers who must rid themselves of everything that may impede the message of the Brotherhood from being universally received and understood, and secondly, that of the brothers who come from elsewhere, upon whom there falls the perhaps thankless task of generously assimilating an ideal of religious life which has not yet existed in their own country. When our Lord inspires a young man with the desire to become a Petit Frère he thereby intends that he should strive to establish the Brotherhood at home. This presupposes great humility, renunciation, and the patience to have the sense to wait until, having assimilated the universal values of the ideal of a Petit Frère, he has become able to work out that ideal in terms of the spirit of his own country and to transmit it to his fellows, without in any way lowering its imperatives. Hours of great difficulty may occur when temptations to discouragement or rebellion will spring up and shake the resolution of a Petit Frère, and his will to persevere until the end. But the bonds of charity must ensure a perfect outcome.

External adaptation to a new manner of living seldom raises insoluble problems; *solvitur ambulando*. The crucial issue does not lie in this sphere; it begins when we try to translate the essential values of the spiritual message and adapt it to a different mentality. Debate begins with questions as to whether it is opportune to undertake some form of manual labour in a particular country (is it not too crude?), whether there should be exposition of the blessed sacrament, whether friendships should be formed without a specifically apostolic aim. In short, everything may be undermined on the pretext of some adaptation that must be made for a particular country or environment. It will be said that this is necessary at the start in order to win acceptance; that we should not rush matters, or cause useless scandal by an ultra modern form of the religious life.

As Petits Frères we must carry out our ideal to the last detail, heedless of the criticisms made by unauthorised persons. Most of these criticisms will be directed against what is considered to be an excess of contemplation in our lives or the way in which we live as the poor have to live. Only gradually will the assimilation take place, and as it were by its own momentum, simply through the presence of some Petits Frères belonging to the country, generously loyal to their rule, utterly self-abandoned, and not over critical of what they have been taught. Adaptation will certainly be necessary, but not compromise. And never, never may we 'adapt' the Brotherhood to every situation and environment and risk destroying the power of a message or the witness to a life which may *not* have been meant to be universally understood, universally accepted, universally fruitful.

It is a strange fact, but one that I have already observed, that some brothers allow themselves to be so easily blinded that they assume the right to bring their brethren back to the practice of poverty, and of universal love and to show them the way to a sounder adaptation to their situation in the world. Their method is to express in the strongest terms their absolute opposition to what is now being done, to formulate judgements that are unjust and to indulge in mere self-assertion. Now I should be the last to minimise the importance of the effort that each brother must make in order to effect those adaptations that are necessary if conditions without which the Brotherhood would not be true to its purpose are to be realised to the full. That purpose is to be a living witness of respect for all men and of unity in a friendship that surpasses differences of every kind. We must love devotedly the country to which we happen to have been 'sent', and this means that we must do our utmost to know, appreciate, and understand it. But this effort must not so monopolise our attention that we become unable to take any interest in other nations and other brotherhoods, that is, in practice, in other brothers dedicated to this work. For this would merely be to substitute one particularism for another, one national egoism for another, and to seal our hearts and minds against the universal claims of love. This twofold ambition of loving service to an individual country and of worldwide love, spring from a single source, a single love, that of our saviour Jesus, whose heart enfolds within an undivided stream of love all nations as a unity, without preference for any one of them in particular, and at the same time is intimately near to each individual man, giving himself in a divine friendship with an amazing care as if the two of them alone existed.

Rome, 7 October 1958

6

The Way of Prayer

We shall not feel that our lives are in any way complete, nor find any peace in our hearts, so long as we are unable to say that we have done our utmost to become abidingly men of prayer.

Prayer holds a prominent position in our way of life, it is even so essential an aspect of it that unless we were convinced that it alone provides a sufficient reason for embracing such a life we should not have the courage to carry on. Is it not the tale of an idiot to embark in this way, in the flower of one's youth, upon a life in which one will do nothing useful by human standards, and very often by the standards of one's own intelligence? Is the thirst we sometimes feel to do something more practical, more directly apostolic, really only a temptation? Should we not achieve a more balanced existence if we gave ourselves to the ministry, threw ourselves body and soul into some activity, than by working as dockers, being brutalised by deep-sea fishing, or looking after herds of goats? What purpose can this serve? And yet there is prayer; there is the hour of adoration; ought we not therefore to live for that alone? In a sense, yes; and also because without it our life could not be shared with our Lord's.

There are, indeed, other reasons for our form of religious life which also are absolute: the love of men, the will to be witnesses of the invisible in their midst, so that through us they may learn to know and to want to love him. This is obvious, and we are very conscious of it: and it is precisely this crazy, apparently useless way of living among them that we could not accept or understand without prayer. It is in prayer that we learn to know our Lord and to keep ourselves united to his intentions and desires.

If our Lord has called us to follow him in this way, does it not follow that he is committed to giving us the grace that is necessary for real prayer? That is true, but it may not involve the totality of the grace of infused contemplation. And yet we must always trust that he will give us *the possibility* of leading our life in union with his, and of sharing the prayer of adoration and supplication with him. But he will do nothing without our co-operation; from the start we must learn to pray, and we must afterwards continue to treat prayer as an important work that calls for our utmost care.

We shall never know whether our Lord has decided to grant us now or in the future this freely bestowed condition of contemplative prayer; it is an uncertainty most trying to accept! Shall we, therefore, in his eyes, be divided into two groups; those who have been called to receive the grace of contemplative prayer, and those who, not being destined to receive it, must perseveringly continue to knock at the door? No, things are not so simple. Our Lord, of course, acts as he pleases; he is the master of his gifts. He comes and goes, visits this man and that, comes early or keeps one waiting a lifetime. But to say that he 'comes' is simply a way of expressing his presence made manifest by a kind of infused knowledge. He has, however, many other ways of being present in a heart that does its best, and gives all its love, in order to reach him through prayer, and yet feels that it never succeeds. He is nevertheless truly there also, although it may prove costly to find him.

Frequently and even normally the course of our conscious relationship with our Lord begins with a stage in which prayer is easier, yielding joy and the warmth of love and an intimate knowledge of our Lord, making detachment a matter of no difficulty at all.

I have described this stage as normal. Will it seem so if we have not passed through it? Supposing we have never experienced this initiation into prayer with its overflowing joy of being with God and entirely under the influence of his activity? Would this be our own fault? Not always. But it may be that we are more or less responsible for this absence of joy, because we have not taken the trouble to learn the right way to pray. Some of you have keenly felt the absence of formation and of a methodical approach in your attempt to live a genuine life of prayer.

There may, however, be a certain amount of self-deception when we throw all the responsibility for the difficulties we encounter in prayer upon a lack of formation or the absence of a method. However fervently we may have prayed, we never reach a satisfying success.

That is the first conclusion we should retain. And we shall be the less satisfied the nearer our prayer has drawn us to God. This feeling of dissatisfaction is, in fact, a constituent of prayer: it is the proof of an unfulfilled desire that can only go on developing as our love increases, and will cease only when we reach the point of seeing God face to face. This thirst is far from being quenched by prayer. Therefore we must be resigned never to feel satisfaction in it, and resolve to seek continually without ever finding, for there is always something better ahead, and its attainment, we feel, depends at least partly upon ourselves, even when God has assumed control and directs our prayer disinterestedly to himself alone.

Prayer means thinking of our Lord with a loving attention. When we pray we learn to know God and to love him more deeply, and even when knowledge is not foremost, even when it is obscure, it is still always there, like an invisible channel through which love is transmitted. Knowledge and love—

yes, but is not this precisely what we seldom experience during those moments we spend in chapel, overcome by fatigue, drowsiness, and routine, moments, however, which draw us back to kneel daily before our Lord in the tabernacle.

There is a general tendency to neglect this *search for the knowledge of God* without which prayer is impossible. May it not be that it is this negligence that lies at the root of that sense of confusion about which many complain while feeling that they are partly responsible for it? Is it not natural that in such circumstances the hour of adoration increasingly seems to be a testing time at the feet of the crucified Christ? It is an hour of the day which has no natural attraction for us, and we find it hard to believe in its utility. Adoration during the night accentuates this impression of a sacrifice offered to God: it is a hardship to get up in the night; the hour of adoration is spent in a struggle against sleep; it is difficult afterwards to go to sleep again, and the effects are felt throughout the following day; one is either always on the point of dropping off, or else one is off colour.

Still we persuade ourselves that we must hold on to this freely given activity, the only one which seems to us to be carried out for our Lord alone, an offering of our time and our weariness, an act of perseverance 'amid the encircling gloom'. Most often no tangible result can be observed, and there is hardly any sense of inner satisfaction. Is not this the predominant feeling which most of you experience? The hour of adoration is an act of courage, of love, of personal attention to God—*it is a sacrifice*.

It is true that all prayer contains this element of sacrifice, but sacrifice cannot be all that it contains. In the long run, unless these courageous acts of sheer self-abandonment, of sheer effort of the will are sustained by a constantly renewed knowledge of our Lord lovingly sought out in faith, they will lead to discouragement. An excessive stress on the will in prayer runs the risk of overlooking the conditions necessary for our self-oblation to God. That oblation must not be a solitary act of courage in the void, but a real committing of ourselves into the hands of our Lord crucified through love. In order to do this, our generous impulses must be directed, in the light of faith, towards his own personality.

What is most lacking when we turn to prayer is a failure to conform ourselves to the laws that govern the virtue of faith and the love of charity. Prayer is nothing but a period especially devoted to bringing into action our gift of faith, with the desire of reaching God through the obscure knowledge it provides, and of loving him more deeply: thinking of God with loving attention.

It is impossible to think of God without knowing him, and this intimate knowledge is wholly contained in the divine faith which leads us through the discovery of our Lord into the very mystery of God in three persons. I emphasise the importance of the act of faith because it constitutes the preliminary action leading to the love of charity. We frequently make the mistake of trying to practise charity without taking sufficient care to give sustenance to our faith. We are inclined to believe that faith can exist and develop without being sustained or exercised by an active intellectual effort. Here, perhaps, is our most serious weakness, and it is only we who can provide the remedy if we want to learn to improve our prayer.

When you so frequently talk about the 'life of faith', does not the phrase conceal some ambiguity? Its content is vague. No doubt it implies a resolution to be true to our Lord, but concern for a clear expression of what this means is missing. Vagueness and a lack of objectivity seem to be symptoms of our time; emotive expressions with a meagre intellectual content seem to satisfy. Every kind of discipline, every external support is mistrusted on the grounds that it is inimical to truth, to personal integrity.

This sensitive anxiety to safeguard one's spontaneity as the basis of authentic prayer acts as a hindrance to the understanding of what real freedom means. This horror of anything artificial, of regulated outward expression, of routine, makes us instinctively reject every traditional support of prayer, every method, every means of disciplining the imagination and the intellect. We seem to be driven spontaneously to simplify the structure of the spiritual life, even that of the chapel and the liturgy, to such an extent that the natural aptitudes for knowledge are deprived of their normal support. The thirst for realism is so intense that from fear of being stranded on the wayside all desire to travel along *any* road is extinguished, and the certainty of straying into a premature void blocking further progress is ensured. This 'void' is not the desert of the absolute at which all roads end, for that is reached only after travelling a long, narrow, and rocky path. Too often this need to feel that they are at one with reality drives modern Christians to bring their attempt to lead a life of prayer so fully in line with the activities going on around them that they look for its sustenance, and even for its expression, mainly from external human contacts that they can actually feel and often leave little room for a direct dialogue with God, a dialogue which can only take place on the level of divine faith, sustained by God himself, by his revelation and the light of his grace.

Have we not all been influenced, more or less consciously, by this mentality around us? We are, fortunately, men of our time and no doubt the same causes have marked us with traces of the same tendencies. We must make use of what is good in them and reject what is erroneous.

We are well advised to become conscious of this tendency to a vague sentimentalism which slackens the discipline of the will. It is a tendency towards reality which, paradoxically, leads us to the loss of the reality of prayer by making us reject the very simple external aids that are essential for human beings. It is a craving for spontaneity which leads us to neglect, if not to reject, the worth of discipline and obedience; and it is the expression of an attitude of mistrust of everything which might tend to create a habit, because habit is mistaken for routine. The truth is, however, that love is impossible without a disciplined will and that faith cannot be developed and maintained without recourse to the humblest means of knowledge, nor the virtues, even the theological virtues, without habits that have been formed by repeated acts.

A prayer cannot be made impromptu: it is too clearly connected with our personality. Our prayer is an expression of what we inwardly are, and it is of necessity intimately related to our general position with regard to God. When we are praying, our faith becomes active in proportion to its previous development in strength and life. If it is to have this freedom of self-expression in an intimate discourse with God, then *its intellectual content must have been sufficiently studied during the time when we are not praying.* Our faith may wither to sterility from lack of nourishment. It is a *living* reality: it feeds on the truths God sets before it, and it grows strong through acts which it lovingly performs. Deprived of food and exercise, a living being is bound to waste away because it no longer assimilates anything.

It is neither logic nor common sense to allow ourselves to be depressed at the spectacle of the feeble state of our life of faith, when we will not make up our minds either to feed or exercise it. It is no real exercise of faith to try to find God, through sheer will-power, in the activities of our own life or through our relationships with other people. It is not from ourselves, not from the depths of our own being that we shall bring forth a life of faith and contemplative prayer, however courageous we may be!

Meditation on the gospel and the scriptures, the reading of the biographies and writings of godly men, theological study, according to each individual's calling and capacity—these form the indispensable foundations of prayer.

I can, of course, appreciate that one may be disgusted by the excess or crudity of some external forms of worship, by their lack of harmony with the more sober and virile style of our own period. But there would be a real danger, in a time like the present, when there is an ever-increasing appeal to the senses through shape and colour, sounds and music, pictorial representation, the cinema, television, and advertising, to wish to dispense with all material presentation of the invisible world where we should always be at home in the full activity of our faith. It would be presumptuous to adopt any other view and take up an attitude contrary to the laws of human nature and to the unalterable way in which God has chosen to act towards us.

It is not enough to provide our faith with sustenance; *it must be made to express itself in deeds*. Has it escaped your notice that it is very difficult to come into God's presence at the beginning of the hour of adoration, if, during the day, we have failed to preserve inner silence, obedience, and charity? Jesus had, in any case, made this very plain in the parable of the publican and warned us that we may not present our offering before being reconciled to our brother.

If we do not bring our faith into action during the day, we should not be surprised that it is fossilised when we come to the hour of adoration. The three spiritual attitudes necessary for approaching God are, so it seems to us, detachment from all things and from oneself, charity towards one's neighbour, and obedience. Not one of these attitudes can be spontaneous; they are habits acquired gradually through consciously repeated acts.

Life implies activity. Living the life of faith involves the deliberate obligation to accept feelings or actions which do not correspond to our ordinary human reactions but which are a logical result of the invisible realities which faith alone can reach. If we are to act against our natural inclinations, we must have a clear reason for doing so, at least implicitly present in the mind, and strong enough to move us to react in this supernatural way.

This task is always difficult to begin with, but it becomes impossible if faith is not explicitly nurtured. We must keep before our eyes the face of Christ crucified or hear his words on the necessity of self-abandonment if we are to be ready to accept any voluntary sacrifice that may unexpectedly present itself during the day. How *could* we be ready to anticipate obedience to our brother superior, be glad to obey, when criticism and rebellion devour us, unless we have in our hearts the memory of Abraham, of Jesus obedient unto death, or of some saint who is even closer to us? In order to harmonise our life and faith, the latter must be *vitually present in our minds, with the power to be expressed in deeds*.

Since prayer is an integral part of our lives, it cannot be better than we are ourselves. It is something we do as Christian men, and the same habits and virtues are at work in the solitude of prayer as in our activity among men in their daily life. Only the object and the goal of our actions differ.

This is what we mean when we say that there is unity between life and our prayer. Each of them needs the other. Every true prayer is *ipso facto* integrated in life. A deliberate attempt to integrate it artificially by giving it motives and directives relating to human interests would be erroneous. When we start to pray we are paying a visit to God; we are at home with him. It is true, of course, that he is present in men's midst and he dwells in every one of them. Each time we act with charity towards others we are united to him. In spite of this, however, he remains transcendently above all created beings, and if we would converse with him and share his intimacy, *we must necessarily put aside everything else*, even men, even angels, even, and above all, ourselves. Hence, it is not sufficient to leave men physically and enter the silent atmosphere of a church or make a deliberate pause in our work; we must turn our minds from everything created, so that there is no longer any barrier between ourselves and God. This means complete detachment from everything and from ourselves for his sake. It also means that when we are praying we must have the power deliberately to put God before all else. This is not a state of mind that we can summon up spontaneously. It has to be acquired through faith daily exercised.

But is it not also true that the company of others, especially those who are in difficulty or suffering, or those who are far from God, moves us to pray and even provides material for prayer? Does not contact with evil make us more intensely conscious of the need for reparation and the urgency of our mission to be standing delegates of prayer? Have not many of you experienced the fact that you were drawn to a greater effort of intercession when you formed part of a brotherhood engaged in the work of the labouring classes.

When we learn to love other men we more easily perceive the need for reparation, intercession, adoration, for the sake of the great multitude who have not received the Good News. 'When he saw the crowds, he had compassion for them, because they were harassed and helpless, like sheep without a shepherd. Then he said to his disciples, "The harvest is plentiful, but the labourers are few; pray therefore the Lord of the harvest to send out labourers into his harvest" ' (Matt 9: 36–7). We are responsible for souls in prayer because our Lord decided that the development of grace in his Church should be related in this way to prayers offered by a great number, and especially by those who have been particularly selected for this work.

Our mission as standing delegates of prayer is a real summons from God. Our Lord's prayer, throughout his nights in solitude, during his temptation in the wilderness, in the hours

88

before he made his choice of his apostles, in the dialogue with his Father on mount Tabor, in the course of raising Lazarus from the dead, in his sacerdotal intercession after the Last Supper, in his lament at the sight of the multitude without a shepherd, in his agonised supplication in the Garden of Gethsemane, in all these prayers as Son of Man for the sake of men, he was doing what was necessary for the establishment of the Kingdom of God among us. They continue to be necessary, but now they must also be offered by his members. We must pray not only in the way he prayed but in union with him, giving ourselves to him in such a manner that he can make his prayer penetrate our own.

It is very evident that Jesus was profoundly moved by every form of human misery, and that he brought the whole burden of their sin and weakness before his Father. But it was truly to his own Father that he was speaking; it was to his Father that he turned when he went apart from men to pray during the long hours of the night. Jesus *saw* his Father with an unclouded vision. That is why our prayer can only very distantly resemble his, and its most perfect form is the offering of our hearts to God in such a way that our Lord may possess them and make his own prayer in us.

How can our contact with others and our love of them assist our own prayer? In the first place, perhaps, because we shall return from sharing their life with a greater detachment from ourselves, more humble and less egotistic, since the same dispositions are necessary for loving God as for loving men as Jesus loves them. Hard and impoverished circumstances are a help towards detachment from self. Our powerlessness to alleviate the moral misery we witness and to provide a remedy for the evil of sin, this very powerlessness forcibly throws us back on prayer, not as a form of escapism that offers an easy solution but because we have gained a more realistic appreciation of the importance of our duty. We also feel the need to appeal to God, to intercede with him, and especially to offer him the suffering that is doubled by the vision of evil and by our impotence to remedy it. Prayer will thus become for us the privileged occasion when we can offer that suffering as a work of reparation.

I am afraid that the omission of the more humble expressions [of prayer] are not simply due to negligence but spring from the more or less avowed adoption of a principle. I fear that on the pretext of avoiding a formalistic attitude and ritualistic routine, we might come to deprive ourselves—and this would be extremely serious—of the elementary means of praying aright. Neglect in small matters is bound to lead to neglect in matters of greater significance. A lack of respect in our external attitude cannot co-exist with an inner sense of that infinite respect we owe to God. For we are human and the unity of our nature is such that our deepest feelings depend upon our bodily dispositions not only for their expression but very often also for a genuine realisation of what they are. The way these feelings are outwardly expressed, as well as the need to express them, varies of course in different races and civilisations. Still, this unity between prayer and gesture is so basically human that the Son of Man himself was subject to it . . . Our Lord expressed his prayer by withdrawing into solitude, prostrating himself upon the ground, raising his eyes to heaven; he also sighed and wept and rejoiced, according to the feelings that moved him during prayer.

[In the course of centuries Christians have increasingly come to realise that their prayer like the prayer of Christ himself and] because of that prayer, is a work of adoration, intercession, and adoration in the name of all mankind.

In our time this awareness has become more vivid than ever, and it has reached the point *when many have come to feel that they must give concrete expression to this permanent commission to pray in the name of mankind by really sharing the circumstances of men's lives.* This new way of imitating the life of Jesus of Nazareth, this summons to be united with that Man–God who was also one of the workmen of his native village, is, in fact, a development in the nature of prayer itself. Our own vocation has followed this course. One of you wrote to me: 'We are the voice of the poor, their liturgy.'

This new conception of prayer owes its origin, and in part its form, to the stark way of life which the circumstances of the poor necessitates, and also to a mentality that has been affected by the new rhythm of modern life. The result of it all is that methods of praying taught by the spiritual masters of past centuries have partly lost their efficacy. For some they have even become psychologically impossible. No doubt this is one of the reasons why many people today find it difficult to achieve recollection and to maintain it. A man who has to submit throughout the year to the rhythm of a modern city certainly experiences the greatest difficulty in controlling his imagination and ideas; worn nerves, constant tension, the fact that he is compelled to receive, half consciously, all day long, a throng of images, sights, and sounds, end by producing a kind of inability to pay attention and to concentrate interiorly. Those of us who have been subjected to the constant influence of such an atmosphere since childhood will find it more difficult than others to be recollected. It is a weakness, an impoverishment of the means necessary for the contemplative life, which we cannot completely remedy. But it would be dangerous simply to accept the fact and do nothing about it.

There are two things to be done: first to react against it to our utmost by preparing ourselves for prayer in the way indicated above, and then when we have generously done all that is in our power, and only then, shall we have the right to offer this weakness as a humble sacrifice to God, begging him to be graciously willing to make use of it as a means of our entry into a prayer of simple attention and self-offering which the Spirit of Jesus within us alone can effect. The gifts of the Spirit have been bequeathed to our soul as a promise of divine assistance when the work asked from us by our Lord is evidently beyond our power. So we must humbly do our utmost to pray aright, beg the Holy Spirit to come quickly to our assistance, and prepare ourselves by a great longing, a patient and trustful waiting for this entry within us of the prayer of Jesus himself.

[We should not therefore] lean on this teaching as an excuse for remaining passive, not learning how to pray, nor reacting against the external difficulties of prayer, difficulties peculiar to our way of life and which we cannot completely escape: fatigue resulting from toil, a chapel that is too small, perhaps far from noiseless, sleep beating us down. But all this will not be a means of purification, a reasonable expectation of a grace of union with God, an offering of a sacrifice acceptable to him, *except on the twofold condition that we have done our utmost to give our prayer the right direction, to make it as perfect an action as possible, and to effect a maximum reduction of the material and external difficulties which are normally injurious to prayer.* For the risk we run is this: spiritual laziness, through its failure to react, may produce a merely passive attitude from which we only try to profit by offering God our boredom.

In order to avoid routine it is wise to vary our prayers; nevertheless, *routine must not be confused with habit.* On the pretext of avoiding routine, some people have been inclined to discard all regular vocal prayer, and all physical expression of prayer: everything physical can indeed become a matter of habit, but since one can also become habituated to making no spiritual effort at all, this line of thought leads only to emptiness and torpor. It is not through giving up the practice of that which at the beginning we experienced as an aid that we shall become more fervent, but by making the daily effort of attention and love that is essential if this practice is to regain its full significance.

Because we are physically oppressed by some form of vocal prayer or by some practice, it does not follow that we should give them up; we should go on making use of them as a sign that expresses feelings we genuinely wish we had and could offer to God. These practices, particularly when they are commanded by obedience or form part of the normal expression of our piety, must not be discarded on the pretext that they involve the danger of begetting routine. An attempt must indeed be made to combat spiritual numbness, but not by discarding vocal prayers or rites which retain their validity, even when the reactions of our senses have become blunted by habit. The liturgy of the Mass, the divine office, the Gospel, the stations of the cross, the worship of the blessed sacrament, are all subject to habit! Does this provide a reason why we should progressively abandon all these forms of prayer? It is illusory to seek a remedy for routine by discarding every kind of expression that can possibly become a habit! An attempt may certainly be made to combat it by introducing variety, but it is far more profitable to ascend to the heights of the spirit and of faith where the realities of the material world may no longer be needed as a sustaining factor but can be used as a means of expression. This was the attitude adopted by the Man-God with regard to the various human means of expression and of material realities, which for him had the function of signs.

We must also set ourselves to attack the causes. For distractions depend upon causes that as a rule are antecedent to prayer: anxieties, worries about our work, misgivings, every incident of our daily life, comes to mind, and with the greater ease because it is precisely when we are praying that our field of consciousness is free from the intrusion of any other activity. When the mother of a family goes to her room in order to read or collect her thoughts, having forgotten to give her children some absorbing occupation, her absence involves the risk of unleashing the hubbub which naturally occurs if a group of children are left together without anything to do. This is the story of what happens to the contents of our imagination when our conscious activity withdraws to the higher realm of the spirit in order to seek union with God. The only thing we can fittingly offer unreservedly to God is our desire to love him, and not every idea that comes into our head. But an attentive heart presupposes an ordinary power of attention in general.

The best remedy for distractions lies in a faithful observance of the preparatory steps that are essential if we are to pray aright: the effort to detach ourselves from what we have just been doing, the return to inner and outer tranquillity, the quickest possible transition from the tumult of our manifold activity to the stillness of prayer. Our memory must be purified by acquiring the ability to postpone the scrutiny of whatever may be worrying us and even the solutions of problems that are pressing.

We must patiently do our best without being over-anxious about the result, a result which in any case we cannot estimate. Only God knows what our prayer is worth. It is wiser not to look back on that prayer in itself, but rather on the way in which we have made a real effort to pray well, on the genuine and heartfelt contribution we have made to this end. When we have done our utmost, all that remains is for us to persevere without discouragement.

The most perfect prayer is not the one in which we think we receive the most. Our Lord so emphasised perseverance as an essential attitude of prayer that we must consider it to be normal that at times we can see no other reasons for persevering than this counsel given by him and faith in his promises. *We must believe that we shall be heard, but it is only very seldom that we can have evidence of this*. But although our prayer at times is primarily a freely given offering of adoration, a surrender of ourselves in faith, or as painful as a sacrifice, it cannot be only this, for it is also the source of manifold grace, bringing enlightenment, knowledge of God, strength, and love. Every true prayer obtains this manifold grace, and we must strive, with all the love we possess, to secure, through this practice of faith which is the essence of every prayer, a deeper knowledge of our Lord, and, God willing, an authentic grace of contemplation.

We have no right, even for the sake of being present in a neglected neighbourhood, to accept a timetable or conditions of work that would rule out the possibility of the normal fulfilment of our obligations to pray. This would be to lose sight of the very purpose of our religious life, and in spite of all our efforts and our goodwill, we should not escape from discouragement, torpor, and even repugnance to that life. Superiors, especially regional superiors, must pay close attention to this question of the organisation of work; it is an important element in our rule, and yet there is a frequent temptation to try to harmonise an overloaded timetable of work with the demands of prayer. On the one hand, we are faced with the desire to identify ourselves completely with the situation of the working classes, the attraction of a craft which we find agreeable, the need to keep in touch with our friends, and, on the other hand, the inescapable demands of a life of prayer, the fulfilment of the obligations of a dedicated life, and fidelity to a solemn promise of obedience made to the Church, the constitutions, the prior of the Brotherhood.

This conflict is real and even comparatively frequent. Sometimes we are tempted to ask whether, as a means of solving it, the Holy Spirit ought not to give us greater freedom in our work of love by bestowing a permanent grace of contemplation in our soul that would enable us to meet the demands of charity without detriment. Why cannot we do what the saints could do? Why, in the footsteps of St. Bernard and the Curé d'Ars, may we not allow men to absorb and consume us, without ever being diverted from the contemplation of our Lord and with the certainty that our prayer is awake in our inmost being, not like a smouldering fire but like a tiny flame, quick with life, activated by all the light and strength of the Holy Spirit?

This truly is sometimes possible. It would, indeed, be paradoxical if religious profession, which is a profession dedicated to perfection, should be an obstacle to the higher freedom under the guidance of the Holy Spirit and to the adventurous living indicated in the gospel which we cannot adopt unless this same Spirit controls us.

The life of religious perfection most certainly cannot be an obstacle to that kind of supreme achievement which God habitually effects in the lives of the saints. On the contrary, it provides the indispensable condition for being at God's disposal in this way; that condition is *obedience*, without which we should be deceiving ourselves.

When we are acting under obedience we may dare all things; if we are not, we can be sure that we are not being faithful to the Holy Spirit, for he cannot contradict himself. He cannot tell a member of a religious order to disregard our Lord's precept 'He who heareth you, heareth me'. Our certainty that God cannot give two contradictory directives, enables us, when we are acting under obedience with an attitude of humble receptivity and abdicating our own judgement, to go beyond common prudence and pursue the folly of the Spirit's wisdom.

Apart from an extreme case like this, it is natural that with the steady spiritual growth in faith and charity, an older religious can allow himself more freedom and act with greater abandon than a novice or a younger professed brother, who in order to remain united to God and keep selfless, needs a stricter and more constant fidelity to the external obligations relating to prayer. Do not make comparisons, do not judge, remember this law of spiritual development, and acquire self-knowledge. You must not anticipate the time when you can dispose of those restrictions which are absolutely necessary for the first stage of the spiritual life. Once again, whatever is done privately and not from obedience, must be considered illusory and lacking in generous self-giving. An attitude of humble obedience is the best preparation for being enlightened by God in prayer.

I cannot conclude this letter on prayer without briefly touching on our periods of *sojourn in the desert*. For these are essential if we are to deepen our life of prayer.

These sojourns in the desert provide some brothers with circumstances conducive to prayer which they could not find elsewhere. These aids must be safeguarded and their proper use understood. In our life they are regular but brief halting stages in imitation of those made by our Lord. But this does not mean that at longer intervals lengthier retreats may not be equally necessary.

If we are to profit from its spiritual advantages, mere bodily presence in the desert is not enough. We must know how to be spiritually present in it so that there we may find God. This spiritual attitude is essential, but as a rule and for most brothers it cannot be attained without a number of external features which together form the setting of a desert. Since it is not often possible to retire to a real desert, its main features must usually be sought in the setting of a hermitage whose position lends itself to this purpose.

Before setting out for a stay in the desert, it is as well to know what we are going to seek. By its very nature, a desert implies isolation, not from men only but from every trace of human presence and activity. By its very nature it is a sign of aridity, of deprivation for all the senses, for sight as well as

D

hearing; it is a sign of man's complete impotence, for it reveals his weakness; in the desert he can do nothing for his own subsistence; and it is the sign of poverty, austerity, and extreme simplicity.

It is God who leads us into the desert, for a man's spirit could not dwell there unless it was directly fed by him. It is this that makes a sojourn in the desert different from a retreat during which it is right to seek all possible means for the renewal or support of faith; conferences, participation in worship, prayers in common, discussions with a spiritual director. Such retreats are necessary and may also involve, according to the quality of an individual's prayer, varying degrees of the solitary life.

The desert is an attempt to go forward, stripped and feeble, deprived of all human support, fasting from all earthly and even spiritual food, to an encounter with God. Of course we shall not be able to go very far unless God himself sends us food, as he sent it to Elijah, lying down exhausted under the juniper tree.

Even when our prayer is the result of the activity of the theological virtues, it always implies a reverential waiting for the food from above. The sojourn in the desert is a trial, a test, like a completely trusting effort to beg God to come and seek us in our helplessness and bring us to himself. *There, what is essential in this sojourn is its total deprivation, its calm and quiet waiting for God, while our faculties remain to some extent inactive.*

This passive waiting, without an answer from God, would be injurious if it lasted long. But if brief, it is most beneficial, like an appeal shouted to God, an appeal we need to make from time to time during our life of prayer. Longer sojourns in the desert should not be undertaken thoughtlessly, nor without spiritual direction, and in any case we should know how to stay there in such a way that we are ready to combine quiet waiting and deprivation with the reception of the spiritual food that is necessary if we are not to die of inanition. This food we should not refuse on the grounds that we can climb the mountain without assistance. For God alone can take us up that height.

Rome, St. Paul of the Three Fountains, 15 November 1958

7

Like a Little Child

How can a man become more perfect *by going back to a state of childhood*?

It is tempting to reduce (our Lord's) teaching to an instruction on the need to be humble, unassuming, and pure, as children are. Humility, obedience, chastity, are surely counsels of sufficient importance that we can accept them without criticism. And, indeed, if our Lord's words only had this meaning there would be no problem. But in that case why did he pick out that little child and solemnly declare that only those who are like it have a chance of entering the Kingdom of God?

We can see at once all the difficulties which a literal acceptance of this teaching involves. Faith is a reception of truth by the mind, and an adult Christian cannot abandon the control of his behaviour by his intellect. For is this not the only way in which he can escape from an emotional and futile piety? Is there not a considerable risk, especially for women and nuns, in taking the gospel counsel literally, and trying to behave like children? Many men, many priests and monks more or less consciously take this point of view. To talk to them about the spirit of childhood merely exasperates them!

I am sure that some of you share this attitude; you are unable to escape from this very masculine and rational outlook which you can easily support by doctrinal teaching and passages from scripture. I have received letters from you asking me to clarify the meaning of this evangelical command.

It is under the influence of the light and grace of Christmas that I want to help you to understand, because if it is true that Jesus made this condition of childlikeness an absolutely essential condition for entry into his kingdom, it would be serious indeed to neglect it! All the more serious, so it seems to me, because our vocation is contemplative and hidden, and demands that in all things we follow him to the end. If perfection may have different aspects, may not the spirit of childhood be attached more especially to the contemplative form of life? Is it not more necessary as a means of entry into the secrets of divine Wisdom than as an instrument of some great apostolic action in the world? 'I bless thee, Father . . . for having hidden this from the wise and clever and for having revealed it to little ones.'

We should all take Christ's warning with the utmost seriousness, for we are still a long way from understanding and practising it.

When he manifested himself to the world, the incarnate divine Wisdom began by being a child, then, having endured the torment of the cross, he won the glorification of his manhood, and is for ever established at the age of divine maturity. These are the stages of the descent of Wisdom among us; the infant in the crib, the man of sorrows, the glorified son of man.

As for us, wretched beings paralysed by the weakness of pride and egotism, it seems that we must take the opposite direction. This does not mean, of course, that we begin with the maturity of glory, but we are in fact first of all attracted, almost spontaneously, by the perfection of a human nature, made anew and maturely perfect. Have we not, in baptism, died with Christ and risen with him again?

When we think of this regeneration of mankind through Christ's victory over death, we are inclined to consider ourselves as already more or less delivered from the tendencies of our unregenerated self and from the childish defects on which St. Paul comments. We are led to stress the exclusive power of our own will and our own courage, and we interpret the counsels given in the gospel on poverty or detachment with the utmost rigour. We believe that if we persevere along this path we are bound to reach perfection and to prove pleasing to our Lord.

At the same time, we tend to judge the moderation and weakness of others with severity, and we criticise obedience whose imperatives seem to stifle our generous impulses. Then we gradually drop our illusions, we come to realise our weakness; maybe we fall. We feel we are marking time, and we thus begin to realise that before we can reach the maturity of Christ, the cross must have engendered in us, year after year, the child who alone is allowed to pass through the gates of the Kingdom of Heaven with Jesus, and so at last to attain the true maturity of the resurrection, which is something quite different from that which we had first considered to be perfection according to the gospel.

We must gradually become infinitesimal in the hands of our Lord, the creator of holiness. The law governing this transformation is that of the gospel, but this was written by the spirit of Jesus, and no one can read or understand it, and certainly not live it, unless he first receives this same spirit within himself. Our mistake is to try to understand the gospel and to put it into practice by our intellectual resources alone, and when we do this we destroy the gospel, for no one can succeed in harmonising in practice the apparently contradictory directives of the gospel of Jesus by the resources of his own mind and will alone, not even when these have been sanctified by grace.

A man who is called to carry out the counsels of the son of God adventurously, to take them seriously and in a sense literally, will fail to do so unless he has agreed beforehand to abandon an excessively argumentative approach which confines him within human limitations, and unless he allows himself to be possessed and led, beyond his own horizon, by the Holy Spirit who was responsible for the gospel and for the apparent contradictions it contains: humility and greatness of soul, tenderness and strength, complete renunciation and the demands of justice, poverty, and an ever-readiness to give, unstinting prayer and a willingness to be at the services of anyone.

In this rule, Brother Charles makes us face all these paradoxes. If, in order to put our Lord's counsels into practice, we have not given up our own system of ideas and our restricted arguments, then what we imagine to be generosity will quickly turn to harshness towards oneself and others, and the gospel of gentleness, pardon, and peace will beget in us demands that have no mildness, an obstinate clinging to our own ideas, a rigidity that will not yield to obedience, criticism of other people, and the Church, and all this in the name of an implacable logic which we call generosity and which drives us to apply the evangelical counsels literally, and not without heroism, but in the light of our own judgement alone.

When we do this we cannot fail, through our behaviour, to contradict one page of the gospel on the grounds that we are practising another! We have forgotten that these apparently paradoxical and contradictory teachings of our Lord are like parallel paths that only meet in the infinity of wisdom and love which are in God. If we lose sight of the point where these paths disappear into the divine infinity, we shall find ourselves unable to follow any one of them without giving up another. Only our Lord's wisdom working in us will enable us to advance towards that perfect synthesis which is exclusively granted to the children of God.

Our Lord's wisdom can act in us only if we allow it to occupy us fully, by a self-emptying and by a most willing docility. Nothing so completely blocks the passage of this wisdom into us as the obstinate clinging to our own ideas and the inflexible attachment to our own judgement. This does not mean that we must have no judgement of our own! Before God we must be like a child; we cannot improve on our Lord's words and when he put a child before us as a model he knew very well what he was doing. The spirit of childhood is beyond our power to achieve, but we are able to initiate its predisposing factors that make the Holy Spirit's action possible. It is the Spirit alone who can give the breath of life to a child of God.

To become a child in the sense that our Lord wishes is not unworthy of adults like ourselves. To think so would be a grievous misunderstanding of the reality of what he intends us to become. It is not a matter of foregoing our reason in the ordinary conduct of life, or of refusing to learn from experience, or of taking the initiative when a decision is required. It means acquiring the ability to see men and things through our Lord's own eyes, and to take into account the realities of the supernatural world he created.

A child has defects, many imperfections, and a lack of experience, and it is not these things that our Lord wants us to imitate. But a child is also a being wholly turned towards the future, a being made to grow. He cannot grow without receiving something from others; and he is only truly developing when he learns how to receive. His normality is shown by the spontaneity with which he offers himself for the instruction and direction which he cannot possibly do without.

Docility of mind and the habit of trustful obedience, even when he is as yet unable to understand, are positive characteristics in a child, factors in his progress without which he cannot develop normally. He is essentially a being that *gives*, and if this gift is to be perfect it must depend upon a fundamental attitude of candour and simplicity. There is nothing more attractive in a child than his readiness to believe what his parents and 'grown-ups' in general tell him and the trust with which he accepts their guidance. A child who has lost this spontaneity has not the same capacity for development in life, his growth will be hampered, full of defects, complexes, and lost achievements. Jesus had seen all this spontaneity and absence of self-consciousness in the faces of the children looking up at him. Only those who look at God in this way are capable of divine perfection. Not our Lord alone but also all those to whom he has committed his authority in the Church are and always will be for us 'grown ups', but we cannot take this view unless we remain, or rather, unless we become, little children with respect to them.

To be 'a little child' is, first of all, to believe that only our Lord knows the way that leads to God, that only he can show it to us and help us along it. The perfection he makes our goal and renders possible by the folly of the cross and the evangelical life is not contrary to reason, but above it, above our own resources of judgement and volition; it depends upon the guidance of the Holy Spirit. To become a little child of God involves adapting ourselves as thoroughly as possible to his guidance, coming to us amidst the light and the darkness of faith. Contact with the supernatural reality of God cannot be made except through the mind's docility to the truths of faith, to the invisible instruction of the spirit, and through the complete abandonment of our own will to the guidance of God thus glimpsed. Docility to the Holy Spirit and self-abandonment to God are the two essential dispositions that constitute a child of God.

Tabris (Iran), 29 November 1958

8

On Obedience to the Church

This letter was written after the events which, in September
and October 1953, led up to the crisis of the worker-priests.
It was during this time that the Apostolic Nuncio requested
the French bishops to withdraw their priests from employ-
ment in work.

Unfortunately, it all too commonly happens that when
events like this occur, free rein is given to the most varied,
most human and sometimes the most violent reactions. It is
difficult for even the most disinterested apostle never to have
allowed some trace, however slight, of excessively personal
ideas and excessively human emotions, to infiltrate into his
apostolate. Who would venture to boast that, in so difficult a
matter as that of the apostolate, he was in possession of the
whole truth, and that his activity had been right beyond
dispute? This proportion of human relativity is the more
likely to be present when apostolic zeal has to be especially
arduous and face situations that are particularly novel and
complex.

Among Christians there is no way of making an absolute
distinction between those who are integral members of the
Church and those who are mistaken. But men of goodwill
exist who strive to attain the truth, and yet do not always
completely grasp it, and who are fallible.

There must be no division into those who have triumphed
and those who have been condemned. And I should like to

emphasise here that the attitude of easy triumph adopted by some who calmly identify themselves with orthodoxy, certain of being in no danger of criticism from the Church because they lack the courage to depart from a facile conformism, is entirely hateful. That kind of judgement already shows that the Church is no longer understood. For the Church has not condemned, she has only issued a warning, underlined a danger, pointed out a budding error, or a deviation already initiated. The soundest, truest, doubtless the most heroic, and certainly the most Christian reaction on the part of those who have been rebuked in this way, is not to set themselves up to judge the measures taken, not to pick out their defects and their human aspects—which cannot be completely absent from any action of the Church on earth—and so, on the grounds of being completely misunderstood, try and escape having to obey, but simply to ask themselves whether in truth nothing in their attitude required revision, and whether nothing in their way of thinking needed correction. Such a complete victory of faith in those who have been thus criticised by the Church is the only means for them to regain the element of truth in their apostolate in its entirety, and to enable it to bear its greatest fruit. Otherwise all is lost.

When we have to face such precise and carefully weighed directives given by the Church, we must always make an effort to grasp what it is he expects from us. This means that we must accept them, humbly examine ourselves, and refrain from criticism of anybody. In her living body, the Church is unalterably one and divine, and we must acquire the ability to appreciate through her action in such circumstances the dynamic impact of the spirit of Jesus ever abiding within her. We must become receptive of all truth, and this we cannot be unless we are utterly humble. In this age of uncertainty the Church stands out more than ever as alone able to safeguard the truth.

It would be to minimise unduly the Church's foresight in the present condition of the world, not to realise at once that she is fundamentally anxious about the hold which the Marxist error may gain over men's minds and about the distorted ideas it may introduce into the outlook of those priests and leaders whose mission it is to establish the Church in the working-class world. This danger is a reality.

I had pointed it out previously, when I explained how, if one allows oneself to become imprisoned in some particular environment, looking at everything from a single point of view, it is possible to lose the faculty of sound judgement with regard to a given human situation. Communism is too important a fact and raises too many problems for us to be able to shirk the effort to see it clearly and to try to understand the implications of our faith in Christ invisibly present in history. What would our Master say to us if he returned now? I believe that he would repeat the gospel, the same gospel, in terms that would leave us in no doubt.

We must be absolutely honest about the teaching he has bequeathed to us. There are pages we cannot tear out, pages from which we must live, even if putting them into practice means weakening the impact and the immediately practical results of the workers' struggle for social justice. There is a radical opposition between the principle of life which is Christ's legacy to us and the single and essential method of Marxism, which is the class war. This is too often forgotten. Two facts exist which cannot in any way be altered: the first is Christ's declaration that the absolute condition for the development of the divine life in man is the creation of world-wide brotherly love, and the second is the Marxist teaching that the one unavoidable method is to intensify the hostility between the classes systematically, until it reaches its violent climax, and that unity is conceivable only within the working class and as a means of combat. I do not wish to dwell on this. I recently sent you some documentation about it.

An initial intellectual confusion has resulted from the Marxist attempt to identify the working-class movement as a whole with the communist technique. A second confusion is due to the fact that there is now a danger of interpreting the Church's reserve as a refusal to give a wholehearted welcome to the working-class world and its authentic aspirations. The initial confusion has made the second possible. The Church is right when she sees great danger in such a situation.

It would be to minimise her understanding of the present state of the world if we did not see the directives she has recently given as primarily an authentic reaction of Christ's mystical body against the gradual infiltration into men's minds of a version of the determinist and materialist idea of the world's evolution, hostile to the attempt to try to adopt Christ's message to it.

In articles published in different papers on this subject I have noticed that views from the most varied circles, from the Left to the Right, from Catholics and non-Catholics, have found expression. It is impossible not to feel misgivings and great sadness when one sees how few there are who will allow that the Church may have acted independently of any political prejudices.

The Church's directives are accused of being lacking in clarity and of having simply broken and dismembered the one missionary movement that was trying to re-establish the Church in the de-Christianised world of the working classes, which increasingly looks like containing the seminal factors of the world of tomorrow. It is easy to conclude from this that once again the Church has rejected the working class, and has refused to incorporate herself in the progress of history, withdrawing, in an introverted way, into a kind of Christian ghetto, and hence linking her destiny with an outdated idea of human society.

That non-Christians should think like this is almost inevitable. But that Christians should also share these thoughts? It is indeed infinitely grievous and even tragic that the Church's action should in fact have affected one of the most progressive and disinterested efforts of the apostolate in the working-class world, perhaps the only one which succeeded in reaching some of the masses who have become widely separated from the Church. But did the Church react against this movement because it was an approach to the world of the workers, or because she sensed that it involved a dangerous departure from the integrity of her divine life and message? The two aspects do indeed coincide, but we must not think that the vital reason for the Church's reaction sprang from an archaic attachment to a political party or to an outdated social system.

As I have already observed, the activity of the Church on earth is necessarily contained within human circumstances, and as it were enveloped by them. Men who are disturbed, who are concerned with denouncing and interpreting, are certainly subject to political and ideological passions which have nothing to do with the truth defended by the Church. This has become all the more possible from the fact that in the social, economic, and political spheres, we often find ourselves today in an equivocal position, with our ideas in anarchy. It is even possible that the Church experiences some difficulty in formulating clearly and precisely the danger about which her divine instinct for conservation has warned her. But the reaction is sound, and is truly that of the living body of Christ. This we are bound to believe.

Never before have I had such an overpowering impression of the extent in which the Church is a mystery and a stumbling block to human reason. She will always remain so, because her reactions cannot be reasonable in the sense in which a rationalist could appreciate them. For in a world without any contact with the universe of invisible things, she has to represent and defend the imperatives of those supernatural realities that are beyond our grasp, and also those that follow from an idea of man justifiable only in terms of an intimate relationship with a mysterious God who is trying to lead men in a direction against which they sometimes struggle with all the resources of a mind whose horizon is too narrow.

I cannot help being reminded of the immense movement of silent and non-violent protest which the powerful spiritual influence of Gandhi succeeded in promoting and maintaining. Gandhi did this through his belief in the strength of purely moral or spiritual values, and the religious soul of his people made the thing possible. Can the priests of Christ allow themselves to be less loyal to the gospel than this, and will they have less confidence in the power of love? The contemporary rationalist and materialist mentality cannot either dispense or excuse us.

The Church also wants to put her priests on guard against an attitude of mind that would lead to the idea that for the time being the gospel is impracticable, and that, at no matter what cost, the first necessity is to change the way in which the proletariat have to live. The gospel can never cease to be both true and possible. But it is also true that a minimum of material equipment is indispensable if a human and Christian life is to be lived. It was this necessity that inspired the Young Catholic Worker's movement, and it is the lack of this minimum essential for a truly human life that constitutes one of the tragedies of mankind. But it never provides a reason for putting the gospel provisionally on one side.

It is erroneous to believe that the abolition of the shameful reality of the wretched condition of the proletariat depends only upon changes in political, social, and economic institutions. Certainly the nature of these institutions is an important factor, even more important today than ever before, but what is even more important is that men should learn the meaning of brotherly love and mutual respect. The best institutions in the hands of unjust and loveless men will beget unhappiness and suffering, while those that are technically less perfect but controlled by men with love in their hearts, who respect the personality of the workers, will perhaps prove to be more effective in promoting the common good. An awareness of the moral and economic position of the various countries of the world will enable this to be better understood.

Because the civilisation that at present engulfs us is one of increasing economic complexity and increasingly material influence, the improvement of social techniques is becoming all the more indispensable. But those who initiate them will more than ever need an evangelical soul.

If, however, we reduce the absolute demands of the gospel with the aim of hastening the establishment of these new techniques, are we not already making a concession to materialism? The Church cannot permit the slightest deviation of this nature in the Christian mind, and *a fortiori* in the mind of those whose mission it is to represent her.

Do we consider that *we* have been completely free from such deviation?

We shall doubtless remain poor, extremely poor, with regard to the social techniques that have to be installed, and the Church will perhaps take less part in them than formerly. But are we sufficiently convinced that those who *are* working to install them need more than ever to draw their life from the gospel? Our mission is to sustain this vital element, through the acceptance of our human poverty, but without any inferiority complex. The existence of such a complex would prove that we still unconsciously believe in the absolute efficacy of social techniques in themselves alone.

The Church cannot allow us to hold this belief, even unconsciously. Some of us, perhaps, have let this inferiority complex get hold of us and so are driven to act in a way that is contrary to the spirit of our Lord.

Was not Jesus, in Nazareth, exactly similar to his fellow villagers, his activities differing in no way from theirs? He could not even perform any priestly action, since he did not belong to the tribe of Levi, and no one knew his real identity. Did not this condition of self-effacement last for the greater part of his life, even though he did not cease for a moment from being and acting as the one true priest?

We share in his priesthood and we live among people who as yet feel no need for the sacraments. Ought we not to carry out our priesthood as he did his, through working for our living, through daily fatigue and daily deeds of friendship? For these were really the only activities by which he could outwardly practise his priesthood. Everything he did as an adolescent, a worker, a villager of Nazareth was in fact an opportunity for that self-offering which was leading to the redemption and formed a preparation for the supreme sacrifice of the cross. Why could not the priests of Christ in their turn carry out their priesthood in the same way, even refraining from acts of worship which the people do not yet ask from them, and by imitating their Master's hidden life among the poor and the working people? In this way the sharing of the worker's toil and hardship would, when this was done by a priest, itself become an authentically sacerdotal life. This at any rate is what some have thought, or have been tempted to think.

The Church, however, tells us that this is erroneous. In the economy of salvation Christ is a priest because he is the saviour. His priesthood and ours are not the same by nature, even though the latter is a way of participating in the former. Christ was saviour *through his very being*, because he was simultaneously both God and man. Since he was God in his being, everything he did, of whatever kind, constituted a series of divine and human actions that were *ipso facto* endowed with an absolutely unique value as adoration, intercession, and offering. This he could not communicate to others, since it was something intrinsic to himself as God incarnate. We are not on that level, and our actions, those of priests as well as of ordinary Christians, can only be proofs of love. But when we give our life-blood, drop by drop in toil—a proof of love—or when we make a total sacrifice of our lives—the greatest proof of love—we can participate in some way in the inner life of our Lord in Nazareth with its immense results.

But the priesthood instituted by him is a participation, not of his being but of some of his powers as mediator. A priest receives these powers so that he may offer the sacramental sacrifice and bestow the divine life through the other sacraments; he also receives the special mission of praying in the name of the people and of proclaiming the Kingdom of God. He cannot renounce these functions without denying his priesthood. It is this that the Church was trying to explain when she declared that it was erroneous for a priest to claim that he was carrying out his priesthood simply by identifying himself completely with the life of the workers. She felt that the seeds of this false view were evident in the practical attitude which some priests had adopted.

It is necessary to be extremely precise about this. For the Church did not mean to say that a priest was only loyal to the priesthood when he took charge of a ministry that enabled him to exercise among the people every power that belongs to his sacerdotal status. But he does have two duties that admit no abstention from their performance: that of offering sacrifice and of praying in the name of the people, and that of proclaiming the Kingdom of God. Thus a priest who neglected prayer and the celebration of Mass, or who systematically refused to proclaim the gospel in any way, on the grounds that Jesus did not do so in Nazareth, would be in error. For the period of our Lord's life in Nazareth occurred before the promulgation of the gospel, and the Kingdom was not then ready to be proclaimed. Now it is different.

It is obvious, however, that there are various ways of helping to proclaim our Lord's message. Some priests are given the direct work of teaching and leading the faithful.

Some bear witness by their special way of life; a Carthusian and a Trappist are also proclaiming the Kingdom, but in their own way. Some have been considered by the Church as exceptionally suitable for being entrusted with temporal works of a scientific or social nature, or for making good some lack in the Christian community, or because an activity of this kind when carried out by a priest acquires the value of an instruction or testifies to the Church's concern. All these activities must contribute to the establishment of the Kingdom of God on earth.

On the other hand, the administration of the sacraments and the guidance of a community of the faithful presupposes that this community exists and that a priest has been delegated by the Church for such a ministry. Even so, although this activity is pre-eminently sacerdotal, it is not indispensable for the fulfilment of a priestly life. Everything depends upon the nature of the ministry which the Church has entrusted to individual priests.

Many priests with a special mission, especially in some regions that are sealed to Christianity, can only carry out their priesthood by their daily Mass and prayer, and proclaim Christ's message only by the testimony of their lives. No priest has the right to give up these things.

In the light of this explanation we shall reach a better understanding of the Church's reasons for warning us of the possibility of a practical or theoretical error that would result from a false interpretation of the mystery of the incarnation and of our Lord's life in Nazareth.

Fairbanks, Alaska, 14 March 1954

PART TWO

Notes on the Apostolate of the Brotherhood

I

The Contradictions in the Life of a Petit Frère

How often it has been my duty to explain to one person or another, most often to priests and even to bishops, the precise nature of the apostolic calling of the Petits Frères. Their poverty and hard work and the invisible power of their eucharistic prayer is understood without difficulty. What does constitute the difficulty, what they find it hard to agree with, is our abstention from the ministry or from organised apostolic undertakings. They ask how such an abstention can be reconciled with the demands of the apostolate in our time, and *a fortiori* with those of a sacerdotal vocation, since some Petits Frères are priests.

If only they would see the reasons for this abstention! When it is a question of Trappists or Carthusians, vowed to a cloistered life for the sake of contemplation and the solemn celebration of the liturgy in the name of the Church, such abstention from external activities raises no problem. But because the Petits Frères are not afraid of living among men and accept the spiritual risks of toil that is often harsh, why, it is asked, do they refuse to become responsible for apostolic activities or the parochial ministry, in so far as these would not be an obstacle to a genuine life of poverty or to contemplative prayer? If we compare these activities, it does not seem at first sight that an apostolic activity of preaching or of the ministry is incompatible with sharing the way of life of the poor and the humility of their social situation.

It will, of course, be granted that such a hidden and silent way of living can be useful and even indispensable for the apostolate in some regions, whenever, for example, a direct presentation of the Christian message is impossible or inopportune. In such circumstances an attitude of hopeful waiting and silent witness seems to be the only possible means of making the gospel known. Was not this the case with Father de Foucauld? In the midst of an almost primitive Mohammedan people he could not have lived in any other way than he actually did. But when a region has become able to receive the gospel message, especially when in the depth of its human hearts there is a more or less conscious expectation of it, how can abstention from a more effective organised activity be justified?

The feature in the way of life of the Petit Frère which will always be disturbing is that it is outside the normal classification of the various forms of religious life. If we want to consider them as contemplatives we shall be disillusioned when we do not find all the conditions ordinarily considered to be essential for sustaining contemplative prayer—separation from the world, silence, the importance of the periods set apart for prayer—present in the Brotherhoods. If, on the other hand, we want to think of them as 'religious' who are dedicated to the active life of the apostolate, we shall be disillusioned by their lack of organisation, their refusal to take on the responsibility of a mission, or a parish, or of some organised activity: in short, we shall be struck by the apparently impracticable nature of their missionary activities.

Does not a life of this kind run the risk of deceiving those souls who are seeking the solid support of the monastic life in order to be united to God and also those who are eager for effective missionary activity adapted to the needs of the apostolate in the modern world?

But the life of the Brotherhoods will not deceive those who are called to it by God, provided their one supreme desire is to belong to our Lord, to love him in their hearts for his own sake, even sharing his anguish for man's salvation. Christ's love for mankind became the permanent source of the apostolate at the moment of his death on the cross; it is there, where the first elements of the apostolate were expressed in the heart of a God in agony, that the centre of a Petit Frère's life is to be found.

A Petit Frère must accept the risk he may incur from the poverty of his means of action, in order that he may keep close to Christ loved for his own sake, and also the poverty of his means of contemplation, in order to remain an apostle amidst those of his brethren who are farthest from our Lord.

The way a Petit Frère thinks and feels is marked by this twofold presence. These apostolic activities are of such a kind that no sufficient justification can be found for them apart from the imitation of our Lord incessantly contemplated in the mystery of his weakness, agony, and death. Should this contemplation of our Lord, loved with an unparalleled love, come to an end, a Petit Frère would find that his life had become meaningless to him, too great a burden and impossible to bear. He would then be in danger of yielding to the temptation of filling his life with more immediately practical activities that could provide him with a centre of interest, in place of our Lord whose friendship would become more remote, and the mystery of whose redemption he would no longer appreciate sufficiently to make it the goal of his life as a man.

But, on the other hand, if a Petit Frère ceased to be stirred to his very depth by the call to work for the evangelisation of mankind, then he would no longer be able to endure the demands made upon him by the more oppressive features of poverty and lowly toil, which is the cost of his presence among the outcasts to whom he is sent.

The ideal of life of the Petits Frères *through its twofold requirement of contemplation and of presence among men, and also through the nature of the means envisaged for carrying it out, constitutes, in fact, a new and original form of religious life.*

The intuition which had driven Brother Charles of Jesus to inaugurate this new kind of life, almost without realising it, by sharing the conditions in which the Toureg nomads lived, had no other cause than an intense desire to imitate our Lord. The Brotherhoods originated in the heart of a man captivated by love of our Lord for his own sake, and who allowed himself to be led by our Lord's spirit all his days. We ourselves will understand this ideal and remain faithful to it, *only* to the extent in which we, too, incorporate all things in a single hearted love of our Lord for his own sake. The light that issues from the contemplation of the heart of Jesus and from our own love of him, alone has the power to illuminate the contradictory aspects of our vocation and to reduce them to unity, in that absence of complexity which in some cases the heart alone can bestow.

2

Nazareth and Apostolic Action

I should be glad if you would share with me some brief considerations on the mystery presented by the years of our Lord's working life, years during which he stayed in his village, without his fellow villagers or his relations ever coming to know, or even to suspect what his real personality was.

The imitation of this mystery was the central point in the spiritual life of Brother Charles of Jesus, and yet at first sight Nazareth hardly seems able to provide an inspiration for a life consumed by apostolic desires, such a life as that of Father de Foucauld.

The imitation of our Lord in Nazareth seems to exclude any deliberate attempt to influence one's environment, and even any testimony one might give as a person 'sent'. For the characteristic feature of our Lord's life in Nazareth lies precisely in the fact that he gave no sign of being charged with a mission of any kind. At no time did he make himself known in any way in his true identity as son of God. His fellow villagers never entertained the slightest doubt about him; he was simply Jesus, the son of Joseph, a carpenter of the neighbourhood!

If we are to live in accordance with this mystery, ought we not to content ourselves with the common round of daily activity, taking care that no evidence of a mode of life differing

123

from that of our fellows is allowed to appear? And, from this point of view, do not such external imperatives as religious celibacy, the common life, lengthy periods of prayer, risk appearing at first sight as the opposite of the ideal of Nazareth? Because of this, some are led to suppress as far as possible every form of existence and every activity that would constitute a departure from the common life around. This goes so far that even the visible nature of the Church and the taking of religious vows is found embarrassing, and the temptation arises even to reduce everything which might be a sign of these things to a minimum. There is a growing tendency to consider that the mere fact of being 'like everyone else' is *in itself* a mark of perfection. This way of putting the life of Nazareth into practice is a reflection of a theory of spirituality, called the 'spirituality of incarnation', which is fairly prevalent today.

We must not, however, interpret the mysteries of Christ's life according to our personal inclinations or with an undisciplined imagination. They should be approached with a watchful respect for truth. Now, of these mysteries, that of Nazareth displays, more than any others, the complete reality and truth of our Lord's human nature. It presupposes that he came among his people as a man like other men and during his youth there was no sign of any kind of his position as Messiah. His life in Nazareth was, in fact, the mystery of an absence of mystery in his human and social life; and it is probably this which is profoundly mysterious!

The consequences that follow from this period of his life are important for ourselves. Our Lord is the Holy One of God. Now this holiness became a reality in the most ordinary circumstances of life, those of work, of the family and the social life of a village, and this is an emphatic affirmation of the fact that the most obscure and humdrum human activities are entirely compatible with the perfection of the Son of God. In the social life of Israel, our Lord was neither a priest nor a rabbi; he did not even follow John the Baptist into the desert. The first element in the spirituality of the Brotherhoods, in relation to this mystery, involves *the conviction that the evangelical holiness proper to a child of God is possible in the ordinary circumstances of a man who is poor and obliged to work for his living.*

In Nazareth, our Lord did not promote any special activity of good works, religious instruction, or the apostolate. Should we conclude from this that we must abstain from all apostolic or charitable activity and do our best to remain submerged in the human mass with as complete an anonymity as possible, and justify this attitude by the silence of Nazareth from which no report of any such activity on the part of Christ has ever been heard?

By nature our Lord was the son of God; his life as a man was simply an addition to that existence. We, on the other hand, with damaged souls and discordant bodily passions, still have the obligation to become sons of God by adoption; the procedure is reversed. Yeast is added to a flour mixture in order to make it rise. With his human soul, Jesus saw God face to face, and only in one aspect was he an earth-bound traveller (*viator*). But *we* are tired or lazy travellers, and in the obscure knowledge of faith we strive to reach the contemplation of God's face; we can only catch a glimpse of it for a moment in that dawn which shone in our Lord's manhood: 'Philip, he who has seen me, has seen the Father . . .' This is why our way is his person, and without his help we can neither live nor develop. Whenever we are called to live and act as sons of God, we discover that we are sick and impotent.

It is within his Church that our Lord has brought these aids into existence. Therefore we cannot be content to be invisibly Christian. We must become visibly, and as it were socially, Christian in the Church, and through her, in the fellowship of the baptised or of those hallowed by religious vows. In addition, we are called to increase this fellowship, and this cannot be done without visible activities or means. No Christian, therefore, may decide to do without them. This is the reason why *it is impossible to make a complete parallel between the life lived by a Christian and that of Jesus in Nazareth, at least as regards their external attributes.* Jesus was an Israelite and in his outward circumstances lived under the old Law whose rules he observed. The new alliance had neither been founded nor proclaimed. The Church had not yet been created, and so the apostolate could not exist. Jesus was neither a rabbi nor a priest; socially, he was just a layman in Israel. We, on the other hand, are now members of a Christ who is risen and who has made himself known to the world, and through baptism we are risen with him. We are visible members of his visible body, and we cannot escape from this condition. All of us participate in the apostolate founded by Christ, and entrusted by him to every Christian.

An over-simplified and literal imitation of our Lord's life in Nazareth as an ideal of perfection might therefore falsify our whole outlook. That life, as Jesus lived it, occurred once only; it cannot be repeated. He remains among men always, but in an entirely different way. We must not be led astray by some of Brother Charles's meditations on the life of the Holy Family; they are the entirely spontaneous, almost naïve, expression of his loving intimacy with our Lord and his relatives who were very real to him. It was something entirely personal, something belonging to himself alone.

We know that in his way of life he entirely submitted to the directives of our Lord whose emblem he bore visibly on his habit, ready to follow him on the world's highways or in the desert in order to share the urgency of his prayer, his priestly activity, his life totally given to mankind: 'In order that the holy gospel may be promulgated abroad, I am ready to go to the ends of the earth and to go on living until the day of judgement.'

To sum up: for the Petits Frères, this mystery of our Lord's life in Nazareth indicates that they are called, at all times, in all places, and in every activity, to take part in the work of redemption hidden in the heart of Jesus, while they remain among men, sharing their circumstances and the labour of the poor . . . Our Lord contemplated and loved for his own sake is the essential constituent of the calling of the Petits Frères.

3

With our Lord in the Desert

Amid the contradictions of their life, the Petits Frères will find themselves unable to maintain their faith steadily focused upon God unless their hearts are firmly detached and inwardly poor. The desert presents itself as a means of attaining this condition, a means providentially incorporated in the life of Brother Charles of Jesus.

Father de Foucauld was spontaneously drawn to the desert, even before his conversion; it was an attraction that corresponded with his approach to God. Later it developed as a result of his desire to imitate our Lord . . . and also through his increasingly urgent need to live with God alone. Nevertheless, at no time did he feel called to withdraw permanently to the desert, far from all human contact; his vocation always stemmed from Nazareth.

It was his destiny, however, to live in the desert more or less all his life, even though his motive for doing so was not to escape from human beings. Each time he penetrated farther into the vast loneliness of the Sahara his aim was to make contact with tribes even more forsaken than those among whom he was then living. Beni-Abbès, Tamanrasset, the Assekrem will always be names that remind us not only of the desert but also of a presence among men. Brother Charles alternated between contact with men (and the requisite preparation for it), and retirement deep into the desert as a place where he could meet his God.

The desert is not a synonym for a retreat. Not every place where a retreat may be held is a desert, and what is usually described as making a retreat is not comparable with a sojourn in the desert.

Every place has its own spiritual meaning inasmuch as it stamps its mark on our spirit through our senses. St. John of the Cross had long ago realised the importance of places as means conducive to contemplation. A desert is not simply a lonely and silent place, like so many places throughout the world, even in the heart of cities. It is more than a place of retreat; its extent and its extreme harshness give it a quality of its own. Simply as a desert it is of no use to man, and the considerable space these arid solitudes take up on our planet seems meaningless in comparison with the less extensive regions that are fertile and over-populated and often unable to provide food for the people who swarm in them. Like the prayer of pure adoration, which it resembles, a desert has no apparent human purpose. It brings man to the edge of his weakness and impotency, and compels him to look for strength in God alone. Israel's sojourn in the desert seems like a test imposed by God upon his people. The memory of the material comforts and of the abundant food they had enjoyed in Egypt tempted them to rebel against the austere freedom to which God was leading them through the purifying tracks of the desert. The journey lasted until Israel had given up its pride when it realised its powerlessness in face of hunger and thirst, and that in the desert the only food it could expect was that given by God himself.

The sign of manna, like that of our Lord's multiplication of loaves, has as its presupposition man's understanding of his powerlessness to supply his own needs. Elijah in his weakness had first to be led in the desert to the very edge of despair before he was given the strength of a sustenance from God that enabled him to carry on to Mount Horeb. It was in the desert that Jesus, having experienced the weakness of human

E   129 nature when faced with the fact that the messianic kingdom had to come about through the cross, and having rejected the mirages of Satan, was divinely strengthened by the angels so that he could set out on his mission.

The Petits Frères are called to imitate the life once lived in Nazareth. It follows that they are also called periodically to spend a certain time in the desert. These periods are especially related to particular happenings in their lives, for example, while they are being trained, or at regular intervals when they are living among men, or more or less lengthy visits made by brothers who feel themselves urgently called by God to intercessory prayer, in harmony with their vocation that has made them co-saviours with our Lord.

The Brotherhoods in the desert would thus appear to correspond to a twofold need which the Petits Frères experience; that of a progressive initiation into contemplative prayer with the ideal of Nazareth as a setting of comparative solitude, an initiation that takes place chiefly in the novitiate houses; and that of a life of adoration and intercession whose intensity demands the absolute solitude of the desert. It is this latter need which is met by those Brotherhoods whose permanent abode is the desert.

The novitiate Brotherhoods will therefore normally be established in desert places, so that the novices may not only lead the working life of Nazareth in them but also be initiated, under the direction of their novice master, into the demands made by prayer and the conditions it requires, through visits to the solitude of the desert of greater or less duration. For Father de Foucauld these journeys through the desert were periods of especially intense union with our Lord: 'As I travel I think of the flight into Egypt and of the yearly visits of the Holy Family to Jerusalem.'

It is with the aim of maintaining this rhythm of solitary prayer that all the Brotherhoods, and especially those established in urban centres and engaged in manual labour, must create a hermitage in their immediate neighbourhood which has all the features of isolation and silence enabling it to be used periodically as a real desert. These brief visits to a hermitage provide the brethren with opportunities for more urgent and intensive intercession. But other Brotherhoods must organise their lives so that they can provide the brethren with the right conditions for a prolonged stay in solitude, and, in addition, the atmosphere of recollection of a fraternal community which many brethren need as a means of renewing their loyalty to their vocation as men of ceaseless prayer.

The apparent contradictions in the life of the Brotherhoods make it difficult for them to fufil their calling perfectly. This is why it is indispensable that those brothers who have lived or laboured in an atmosphere of materialism should be enabled to find not only desert places conducive to prayer, but also real Brotherhoods that will provide that atmosphere of recollection, prayer, and adoration of the blessed sacrament which they need. It is to such Brotherhoods that those brothers who have a special calling to prayer in solitude may rightfully be drawn. In this way the Brotherhoods of the desert are closely linked with those elsewhere in carrying out their common vocation.

We must now ask what the spiritual outlook of those brothers called to spend a more or less lengthy period in the desert ought to be.

The prayer and charity of the enclosed monastic orders and of hermits has, as a result of the communion of saints, never failed to influence the life of the Church as a whole. But contemplatives only gradually came to realise, as the Church developed through the centuries, their hidden part in the redemption of their brethren and in the apostolic life of the Church.

It is clear that the Petits Frères have no call to live

permanently a life of solitude in the desert, or as monks with separation from the world as an essential element in their pursuit of holiness. We shall see how the fact of remaining present in the world is a fundamental implication of the Brotherhood's vocation. The periodic visits of the brethren to the desert must be envisaged in the context of the fulfilment of their calling to a mission of adoration and intercession. This is another instance of the way in which the basic outlook of the disciples of Father de Foucauld and that of St. Teresa of the Child Jesus are the same. It is a work of love involved in the quasi-pastoral charge of men with which we are entrusted, so that we may bring their sufferings and petitions before God, in union with our Lord's prayer in the desert. One and the same motive drives a Petit Frère to come down and mingle with the human multitude or to climb the mountain, alone, to meet the God who saves him.

Our Lord's visits to the desert were intimately connected with his mission as a saviour. It was in the desert that he confronted the total cost of that mission: the proclamation of the gospel and his death for his people and for mankind. The nights he spent in prayer, amidst his crowded life, also formed part of his mission as a saviour. This prayer, together with the adoration of his father, is the complete expression of his function as redeemer, incorporating the totality of his mission and his responsibility for the salvation of mankind. The temptations to which he was subjected by Satan prove this, and also those nights of prayer before he chose his apostles and in the Garden of Gethsemane. This was prayer in its absolute reality; our Lord was alone, neither eating nor working, alone before God. The apostles and the saints chosen by God for some great work of evangelisation experienced similar states of prayer: St. Paul in the Arabian desert, Francis of Assisi in his various hermitages, especially at Alverno.

Ceteris paribus, this stark and solitary prayer is that of the Petits Frères whose calling commits them to share, through solitary prayer in the desert, the vocation of those engaged in the mystery of the redemption of mankind. It is, in fact, a real culmination of their apostolic calling; it presupposes death to self and a generous commitment to every demand made by our Lord's love for men; it means that the salvation of humanity has become their life's main concern . . .

If the desert is to become a pathway to God, it must be welcomed by a mind that has really abdicated worldly desires. That inner stripping of desire to which our poverty should lead us is now a necessity if the desert is not to crush us but become an emancipation in our journey towards God. It is also in the desert that we can make a periodic clearance of those illusions which prevent us from obtaining a clear view of all the things that clutter up our heart. Travelling in the desert soon becomes impossible if one's heart is not open and unattached, and if one continues to expect from life something other than God alone. This is why temptations to make ourselves useful to men in any other way than by the affirmation of the divine transcendence through the example of our lives, the temptation, for instance, to establish God's reign by any other means than those employed by our Lord himself, can ultimately only be overcome, as our Lord overcame them, in the desert.

4

With our Lord among Men along the World's Highways

When they come back with our Lord from the desert, nostalgia for God must haunt the hearts of the Petits Frères as they travel among the human multitude. They will be poor in all things except God, and be of little apparent use, sharing the weariness of those who labour, their sole purpose being the proclamation of the saviour's gospel. They will submit their thoughts and deeds to the divine friendship in order that they may make known to those around them the infinite mystery of that friendship towards men, hidden from all eternity, but revealed to us in the heart of Christ. 'And in the morning, a great while before day, he rose and went out to a lonely place, and there he prayed. And Simon and those who were with him followed him, and they found him and said to him, "Everyone is searching for you", (Mark. 1:35–8). 'Then he went home; and the crowd came together again, so that they could not even eat' (ibid., 3:20).

Our life is marked by an alternating rhythm, a movement in opposite directions, imposed by our vocation. We turn away from the world to solitude, for the prayer that will equip us for our work with men. We turn away from men with their pressing need for friendship, to the desert, in order to find God there. No doubt it would have been simpler to have remained in the desert, and there maintained the ideal of poverty, prayer, and love, of which we have spoken. Had we done this we should have followed the footsteps of St. Teresa and many other friends of God.

We know, however, that God asks us to live among men, and in doing so he understands the risks to which he exposes us and all the problems that are bound to arise in the Brotherhoods. It must be made unmistakably clear that problems of a practical nature that occur in our vocation can receive a satisfactory solution only when they are considered from the lofty viewpoint of contemplation. A Petit Frère who had lost sight of the transcendent and supernatural nature of his calling would be continually coming up against objections, provoked by a solution based upon a scheme of things not broad enough to allow for that complete liberty of the divine action, which even in the case of Christ himself imposed limitations involving weakness, abjection, and contradictions. In order to reveal his mystery, God sometimes chooses human lives which, inasmuch as they loyally submit to the spirit's guidance are 'folly to those who are perishing, but to us who are being saved it is the power of God' (1 Cor. 1:18).

From the start, we must have a sure grasp of the real level at which our vocation is to be carried out; otherwise we shall not be able to understand it. The simplicity of the supernatural intuition which gives us the certainty that the Brotherhood's way of life, as handed down by Brother Charles of Jesus, is authentic, must not prevent us from inquiring into the chief reasons that led providence to bring it into existence in our time in order to meet a need of the Church's apostolate.

A prophet is brought back from the desert into the public arena only when there is a mission for him to fulfil. *Nothing less than an urgent call to evangelise the world can justify the pursuit of a contemplative vocation of intercession outside the desert.* We should hold this with absolute conviction. We are called to a mission of intercession through prayer and the offering of our life as a sacrifice, but we are also called, in so far as our lives are spent among men, to an outward mission of evangelisation. These are the aspects of our mission to which we must now give definition.

We have shown how wrong it would be to make the exclusive and as it were literal imitation of a limited period of our Lord's life, even if this includes the long years he spent in Nazareth, the sole purpose of a religious way of life. Although it is true that the Brotherhoods' way of life takes its inspiration from the mystery of Nazareth, we may not consider this mystery apart from the present existence of the risen Christ whose members we are, marked with his seal and invested with the common obligation of bearing witness to the faith and the apostolate.

The imitation of our Lord in his journeying along the roads of Palestine, amidst the crowds who thronged around him and would not let him go, in no way implies that the Petits Frères are called to be responsible for the ministry of preaching and of the sacraments, or to devote themselves to works that alleviate human suffering. Our Lord had compassion on the multitude who are like sheep without a shepherd, like starving men to whom nobody gives bread, and yet he did nothing to accelerate the slow growth of the mustard seed which he planted deeply in the earth, without apparently worrying about the intervening generations that were bound to follow each other before this tree had grown large enough for its shade to cover the world.

Every member of the Church is given a special task by our Lord to which he must remain humbly faithful for the good of the progress of the Kingdom of God. No one can undertake everything, nor cope with unlimited needs, and no one has the right to abandon the mission assigned to him by providence and the Church on the pretext of meeting immediate needs for which he is not directly responsible. St. Teresa and

Brother Charles of Jesus felt this so strongly that they tried to satisfy their boundless ambition that was for ever widening the field of their apostolic desires, by turning to another realm than that of their human condition . . .

So absolute a desire for boundless action in time and space is the sign of a contemplative vocation and it can be fulfilled only through co-operation with the activity of God himself. All outward activity, even if it is apostolic, leaves such souls unsatisfied. A desire of this kind can only find fulfilment in a vocation of intercession. We certainly shall not find it in the necessarily limited activity of our own modest apostolate of evangelisation. So we have no choice; we must either agree to give ourselves generously with inexhaustible zeal to our vocation of prayer and sacrifice, or accept the dwindling of our aspirations to the narrow limits of a respectable suburb or of second-rate professional activity. We cannot tolerate the restriction of our outlook in such a way, and yet its possibility is a danger that lies in wait for any Petit Frère who is insufficiently aware of his vocation to be our Lord's companion in intercession and sacrifice. This is what the glorious name of 'Petits Frères de Jésus' should mean to us.

Our human activities are limited and often intrinsically uninteresting, so that our natural need for creative activity is very likely to remain unsatisfied. The activities of a Petit Frère really do not add up to what is requisite for a well-filled life! From this point of view it is a vocation that demands the prospect of eternity, similar to that of a cloistered monk.

The consequences of this poverty will, however, most often be concealed, especially at the beginning of religious life, by the attraction we experience from a new mode of existence that sometimes has the appearance of a somewhat spectacular—why should we be afraid of the word?—brand of material poverty, or even more, through being apprenticed to a trade, or through becoming acquainted with a new country. These are factors that can sustain for some time the need for self-giving which is natural to the young. It may be an illusion at the start, but there is no need to worry, so long as the soul remains generously faithful to its vocation to prayer and submissive to the spirit who will lead it gradually through successive renunciations, in humble obedience, to a state of prayer motivated by faith, in an ever-closer union with that of our Lord. This inner progress, by slow stages, towards the discovery of a hidden life of prayer is one of the chief signs of a vocation to the life of a Petit Frère de Jésus. Through the clarity of this inner vision we can now understand how our way of life transforms us into real apostles.

The Brotherhoods' position in the Church is very humble, and their way of life must not be interpreted as a criticism of or a failure to appreciate the other forms of the apostolate of which the Church approves. At the same time the apostolate of the Petits Frères seems to meet a new need for the evangelisation of the world which it is well we should realise.

Mankind has never had a greater need for a Christian soul. And yet the earlier success of missionary work seems to be petering out, as a result of the new conditions of life due to social or international upheavals. The development of technical methods penetrating even into the spheres of sociology, psychology, and education, has stimulated the desire to apply these same techniques to the apostolate.

In addition, mankind is troubled by an intense desire for unity, collaboration, and emancipation in order to avoid the most appalling catastrophes. This has led Christians to emphasise in their apostolate the significance of justice, peace, and fraternal love. Nostalgia for unity is driving the Christian bodies separated from the Church to draw together, moving them to minimise their doctrinal differences or to make them of secondary importance. A general tendency among the various religions or ideologies displays itself as an inclination to consider differences in belief and dogmatic truths to be of less importance than unity of action for the attainment of peace.

Discouragement and scepticism are driving mankind to seek a solution in an intensive development of material well-being. The existence of an invisible world, or of a super-terrestrial destiny, seems to arouse far less interest. Influenced by this contemporary mentality, generous hearts are inclined to look for Christ in the happenings of our time, in the working out of history, or in a quasi-exclusive service of mankind.

Christians who are passionately concerned to remain in close contact with the world are especially liable to become victims of these trends. But the intellectual content of these spiritual ideas, aimed urgently at practical results and filled with generous desires, is difficult to define in terms of objective truth. Amidst it all, the Christian apostolate, enriched by fresh points of view and having re-acquired the sense of community, is in danger of one constant temptation: that of neglecting the teaching and the living presence of our Lord who in the end must be met by every human soul, and whose return to us forms the centre of the world's history and of its final transformation. In this context the timely nature of the message of Brother Charles of Jesus calling us to the apostolate of witness through the humble means indicated in the gospel can be more easily appreciated. This way of proclaiming the objectivity of the invisible world has come at the right time and, in its lowly position, to be incorporated in the great general movement of the Church's apostolic activity. Jacques Maritain once wrote: 'In a time like ours, the Christian community faces two opposite dangers: that of seeking holiness only in the desert, and that of forgetting that holiness needs the desert.'

Is it not true that one of the results of the way of life of the Petits Frères is to assist the Christian community in avoiding this twofold danger? There is no need to dwell on the reasons —they are too well known—for the divorce, in the modern world, between human life and the transcendent reality of our Lord's reign which, even so, is still coming into existence in the Church and the deep places of the human heart. These Brotherhoods which are faithful to their ideal meet this vital need in two ways: by the practical result of their example, and by a spiritual doctrine of sufficient force to maintain a contemplative existence in the very midst of the world. We do not perhaps sufficiently appreciate the vital importance of a testimony of this kind.

One of the results of the religious life of the Petits Frères is precisely to show, through their practice, that authentic contemplative prayer is a possibility in the same circumstances as those of the wage-earning manual labourers who bear the heaviest burdens resulting from the advance of technical civilisation.

The effort made by each of us to remain courageously true to our union with Christ, in spite of all the temptations, the tedium, and the fatigue of a brotherhood sharing the world's work, has its repercussion upon all the members of our Lord's mystical body. All the workers, imprisoned by industrial toil, worn down by excessive fatigue, all the poor who are exhausted by anxiety for their daily bread, all those whose mental energy and moral conscience are dissipated in a civilisation organised for pleasure, rediscover something of their belief in God and of their union with Christ, through contact with the Petits Frères and with their contemplative prayer. A brotherhood that is true to its vocation of prayer in poverty and toil can have an influence upon Christians who are near them or who come to learn of their existence that is far beyond what one would suspect. Is it not true that the mere example of the Brotherhoods has many times contributed to restore to laymen, and sometimes even to priests, the meaning of the prayer of adoration or of God's presence in their lives?

A perpetual cause of astonishment produced by the existence of a zealous Brotherhood is due to the fact that men who are thoroughly capable of 'doing something worth while' are content to spend their lives in this way, doing nothing of interest, and with no purpose that can really satisfy the legitimate aspirations of a normal man. It is a renunciation that is a sign enabling men to suspect that a supernatural reality exists in the invisible world. In fact, if that world is unreal, a way of life of this kind is inexplicable.

Without the living example of the Brotherhoods, many Christians would not have believed that authentic contemplative prayer is attainable in the ordinary circumstances of modern life, and they would not have dared to think that it is a vital need for them personally. There are testimonies in plenty that make this plain. Although the chief lesson of the religious life of the Brotherhoods springs from the eucharistic prayer of adoration, the testimony of their poverty and their brotherly friendship must be added to it.

The evangelisation of the poor is one of the signs of the coming of the Kingdom of God which our Lord mentioned to the messengers sent by John the Baptist. It is for this reason that the Petits Frères decided to make their approach first and foremost to those who are farthest from our Lord and who are most abandoned, in order to demonstrate our Lord's love for them in its deepest aspect as a real divine friendship. Is not this choice of the poorest of mankind an initial indication that our way of life is in conformity with the gospel? Brother Charles of Jesus, in his directives for his Petits Frères, had laid down the conditions to be observed when deciding on new foundations: priority should be given to the establishment of Brotherhoods in countries that have not yet been evangelised, and especially in those regions to which access is most difficult, where the people are derelict, and where danger is a possibility.

Thus the selection of a place for a foundation is not determined by a concern for efficiency or by any legitimate apostolic strategy, as, for instance, the choice of a particular group of people whose development might influence the rest of the population. The Petits Frères must, on the contrary, allow themselves to be guided by a determination that no man, no group of human beings, even though they may constitute only a very small minority and be entirely without influence, shall be left on one side. The absence of human development, remoteness, geographical inaccessibility, these provide sufficient justification for the presence of a Brotherhood.

If the love of God must form the invisible content of the Petits Frères' life, their outward activity and the way they live must be entirely motivated by their friendship for men. For most men it is difficult really to believe that there is any evidence that God shows personal concern for them. Evil, suffering, and death form a screen between man and God, and make the mystery of the love that is hidden in God hard to appreciate. And yet, now as never before, mankind needs to believe in the divine friendship, and not merely in a general and impersonal kind of love with which God may be presumed to bestow upon everything he has created. His love for each individual human being is a friendship of the greatest intimacy, calling every man by his own name. How is it possible to believe this to be true? Even our Lord's sufferings, his agony and death, which are like God's ultimate attempt to make himself understood, do not always succeed in convincing those who are disillusioned, indifferent, or in rebellion against the evils and wretchedness of their lives.

How can the faith be taught to a man who has not at least begun to suspect that he is loved with God's friendship? If the Brotherhoods are sent ahead of those who will come later, in the name of the Church, to evangelise by the word, this is in order that they may teach men to believe in the reality of God's friendship for them. Without their hearts being prepared in this way how could they be able to see the proof of love that shines through the story of Christ's passion? A man, especially one who has been hardened by toil, injustice, or extreme poverty, needs to come across some obvious manifestation of love, if he is to believe in it. The Petits Frères must show themselves to be the manifestation of this love to mankind.

Our Lord has asked us to love men exactly as he loved them, and the Petits Frères' way of life might be summed up by saying that they must do their utmost to ensure that what they feel, what they do, and how they live, forms as perfect an expression as possible of our Lord's own feelings towards mankind. This mission is so absolute that everything must be subordinated to it. To love as Jesus loved means to love with an infinitely respectful friendship, with a complete and most humble self-giving. This is the essence of the matter, and the Brotherhood's way of life gets its whole definition from its relationship to the commands of love; it must be a manifestation of it that is as pure and perfect as possible.

When a friendship is profound and exclusive, it demands *the presence* of the person loved and a mutual *sharing*—as fully as this may be attained—of the particular circumstances of life and especially of any suffering. It must also involve a total and disinterested gift of oneself to the person thus loved for his own sake with a humble respect, in the way God loves each one of us. These demands of friendship define the essential elements in the constitution of a Brotherhood.

The Word embraced every aspect of human life except sin, and he came to dwell among us, at Nazareth, in a human family and a human community. This presence in fellowship with others is certainly the first of the requirements of love which seeks to be near the person loved and on a certain equality with him. Presence is also the preliminary condition of all human intercourse, of every kind of transmission of truth and life. In order to bear witness, in order to teach, it is first necessary to be among men and present to them, not only in body but also in heart and mind. Presence among men is like the answer to the first part of Christ's command when he instituted the universal apostolate of the Church by sending forth the apostles and dispersing them: 'Go. . . .' The gift of tongues made the need for a completely intelligible contact finally clear, through enabling the apostles' preaching to be understood by everyone. To establish and maintain contact with men for friendship's sake, in order to know them and be known by them, visited and disturbed by them, in season and out of season, is a work, therefore, that makes great demands.

Our own special vocation is to bring this presence into existence as fully as we can, modelling ourselves on our Lord's life in Nazareth, by coming to live among those who have been entrusted to us by him, in order that we may love them in his name. A Brotherhood must be housed in a dwelling among other dwellings, and the Petits Frères must accept the risks of inconvenience, noise, and swarming people, as a work of love and a proof of their friendship.

It is this that gives them the right to count on our Lord's help which will enable them to persevere in prayer in spite of these difficulties and will transform the poverty of the means at their disposal into an instrument of detachment and purification. This literal dwelling among the poor is a necessary element of our vocation; through it we become their guests, and we put ourselves in a kind of dependence on them. This bodily presence would be insufficient were it not completed by a profound spiritual presence also. It is a *human* presence, achieved through the adoption of their language, and the progressive assimilation of their culture and mentality in all its elements that are true and compatible with religious and Christian perfection. For some this desire to be present and to give themselves may even lead to a request for naturalisation.

The achievement of so total a presence in relation to those to whom God has sent us can, itself alone, involve the work of a lifetime, and presupposes a more thorough detachment than might be imagined, especially during the early years. But even though it is an adaptation that may provide sufficient to occupy one's whole life, it must always be carried out with humility and with the single aim of making it a proof of our friendship for men, and through this, of the truth of our love for God.

This sharing of the circumstances of life of the poorest of mankind with all its implications—working daily for a living, uncertainty, privation, being tied down to an inhuman job, suffering of all kinds—is a way in which a Petit Frère can prove his love. It is a state of life which may sometimes be burdensome, but we should remember that we chose it freely, and that there can be no divorce between our love for our Lord and that which we devote to our brethren. We shall be able to practise poverty and accept its consequences only if we are motivated by love: 'My God,' wrote Father de Foucauld, 'I do not know whether some people can see you poor, while they deliberately stay rich . . . But for myself, love is inconceivable without a longing, a longing to share the circumstances of [the person one loves] and to become like him.'

Sharing the life of the poor is thus one of the obligations of friendship towards them. But it cannot bear fruit if we fail to find in the burden of our daily work a means of entry into our Lord's own work and of carrying our cross in his footsteps. This is a further example of the way in which the sharing of work may sometimes provide the evidence for a love that is eminently devoted and complete, for instance, when the Petits Frères feel called to take part in work that is particularly difficult or dangerous, such as mining, some of the chemical industries, or deep sea fishing.

It is friendship also that will move a Petit Frère to wish to devote himself to prisoners, even to the extent of sharing their imprisonment. There is no better example of the deepest aspect of a Petit Frère's vocation: presence through friendship.

Some people, obsessed by doing something that yields immediately practical results, will ask what purpose such a presence can really serve? Prisoners, they will say, need to be instructed by sermons and supported by the sacraments; and this is the duty of the chaplain. They also need to be given material assistance and educational facilities in their spare time, and informed about the welfare of their family; this is the duty of social visitors and prison helpers. Of what use, therefore, can the presence of a Petit Frère be? Only this: it proves that he loves his friends in prison even to the extent of wanting to share their detention, and that through this friendship they may be led to discover God's friendship for them. It is an inestimable boon for a man to be able to feel that he is worthy of being loved for his own sake, and that he has the power to give joy to another person by giving him his friendship.

Others, though never the prisoners themselves, will object that this is not a genuine but an artificial presence, since the Petit Frère is not really a prisoner and is only in prison as a result of his own free choice. The same objection is sometimes urged against Brotherhoods who are labouring with the working classes.

Now it is true that it is an unavoidable aspect of the Petit Frère's presence among workers or prisoners that it is the result of their own free choice. A Petit Frère need not be toiling at a given kind of work, or need not be in prison; his decision to be there was taken freely. He is not exactly in the position of any other prisoner or worker, but he is all the more their friend because the essential element of friendship is that it is freely chosen. Sharing the circumstances of another's life to the utmost is a work of love; if it is not that, it is nothing in itself, it has no meaning. One may be troubled by being unable to identify oneself completely with the person one loves; but this difference that remains because no further advance is possible, in no way diminishes the value of the witness given to friendship. It may even enable the generosity of a friendship which is unafraid of going to the extreme limits of physical and moral possibility, to be more easily understood.

To love someone with the love of friendship involves the pursuit of that friend's welfare and giving it precedence over one's own. Too often we estimate the worth of a friendship by the feelings, frequently overcharged with emotion, which it provokes in us. But when, as in the case of Brother Charles of Jesus, love creates the need of becoming like one's friend, this is in order to draw near to him and make the gift of oneself a possibility. It is definitely not for the sake of the personal pleasure that such an experience may provide. This may profitably be mentioned, especially for the benefit of those who, in the generous enthusiasm of early years, are approaching a people whom they wish to love devotedly.

In the long run the greatest good of those we love can only be the possession of our Lord himself. This is our friendship's keenest desire. But it may be that our friends do not share our thoughts, and in their view the natural expression of friendship is of a quite different kind; it is related, for instance, to material advantages, the alleviation of disease, or the education of children. This difference in outlook may produce real difficulties and a misunderstanding which we should appreciate and bear with patiently. A friendship that is completely reciprocal requires a kind of equality on both sides; both must stand on the same ground, and together seek the same good which they will mutually share. Without this, no real friendship as yet exists. Until it does, we must wait with humility and a respect for others that is all the greater because they cannot yet see and desire the true good, that which is *the* truth and *the* life. We should take pains to understand the necessity and remember that although our Lord has called us his friends, he must often have felt that he was far removed from the concerns of even his closest disciples! Some of his remarks betray the fact that this lack of understanding was a burden of great sadness: 'Have I been with you so long, and yet you do not know me? . . .' (John 14:9). But this did not stop him from continuing to act as their friend, telling them all the secrets he had learnt from his father: 'No longer do I call you servants, for the servant does not know what his master is doing; but I have called you friends, for all that I have heard from my Father I have made known to you' (ibid., 15:15).

Our friendship for other men must be like that of our Lord. It must always be *infinitely respectful* towards them all: this, in my view, completely sums it up. God alone is Father, for he alone is the real owner of all things, and therefore he alone can give what is his by right. Even the priesthood itself cannot make a priest into more than a very defective instrument; nothing is more distressing and more opposed to our Lord's attitude than that sense of superiority which we sometimes take to be legitimate because it is based on the possession of the faith. We have a quiet conscience because we give thanks to God for this gift . . . But did not the Pharisee whom our Lord rebuked do the same? He was righteous, but he aired the fact, and contrasted his case with that of the poor man, the poor and humble sinner. I want to emphasise this with absolute conviction, for I believe that should our hearts cease to be humble and properly respectful towards every man, whoever he may be, our vocation will have lost its meaning, since our apostolate consists in making our Lord's love for the poorest of men blazon forth *through our lives*.

Be scrupulous, even intransigent, be severe with yourselves on this point of respect for others and begin by respecting those brothers with whom you are living. Impatience and anger are less grave and less wounding than irony or contempt. Jesus broke out in anger, but he never allowed himself to be witty at another's expense. Contempt would have been a contradiction of his creative and redeeming heart, and yet he had a more realistic understanding than we have of the weakness and evil concealed in the human heart under the appearance of good. He had no need of instruction on this point. But the sight of evil and of the most hateful treachery only made him infinitely sad, and he wept.

It is a great thing to find a heart that is always attentive and respectful to others, to all others, that never condemns or judges; so great a thing, indeed, that only God can have fashioned it. Even though you may give all your time, even though you spend yourselves to breaking point, even though the purpose of this devotion is a work of the highest importance, such as that of evangelisation, it is all worthless and Christ's love is not in you, if your heart is not filled with respect for all men, for the least of men, for those who do not understand you, for those who repel your advances, for those who are your enemies and are wholly unlike you. A man who does not realise this obligation, who fails to observe whatever may be contrary to this fraternal respect in his words and in his approach to others, and is not troubled by it, is unable to be a Petit Frère, and has not been called by our Lord to follow this vocation of worldwide fraternal love. Father de Foucauld laid it down in his rule that the Petits Frères must be the friends of all the world, 'Universal Brothers'. The Brotherhoods must therefore be wholly motivated by this love, or at least be constantly trying to become so, otherwise they will become useless, and no longer be anything real at all. But provided they are faithful they will, in spite of appearances, powerfully contribute to the advancement of our Lord's reign on earth, and among peoples the most opposed to each other.

We shall be the more inexcusable for having failed to understand this obligation that flows from love, because of the fact that God has put at our disposal a privileged means of fulfilling it, by dispersing the Brotherhoods in an astonishing way throughout the whole world among the most varied peoples, races, and environments, and thus enabling us to feel, as it were in our own bodies, the repercussion of all the contempt, hatred, and indifference that pervades the world, especially with regard to the least of those 'little ones' who are most loved by our Lord. It is this which explains the site chosen for certain foundations; our Lord's love is of such a nature that it can mobilise everything that is worthwhile and all the resources of the earth, in order that they may be laid respectfully at the feet of a single man, even if he is entirely primitive, completely derelict, socially useless, and apparently hardly human. Should the day dawn when the Brotherhoods begin to choose the sites for their foundations with a view to the possible influence they may yield, to the detriment of people who are complete outcasts, on that day they will also have begun to be unfaithful to their vocation.

On the other hand, we must remember that others must act in a different way, for the Church has received the command to evangelise the world through every legitimate means of instructing the mind and convincing the heart. If the infinite and undivided richness of God's love for mankind is to be expressed in human language, it demands a number of different approaches and ways of feeling to respond to it. It is too great for the heart of any man to have the power to express its amazing variety and fullness. That is why there is an infinite number of possible vocations that can contribute to the expression of this single divine love: they will never exhaust its mystery. For each individual, therefore, it is a question of his own calling, and God calls as he pleases. As for us, we have to pay careful heed to the call addressed to ourselves.

5

Silent Witnesses to the Divine Friendship

If the real welfare of our friends lies in the knowledge of our Lord, why do we not proclaim him, in St. Paul's phrase, in season and out of season, why do we not go into the public places and assembly rooms, and wherever there are human beings and cry out our faith? What is the reason for this silence? Why are we content to reveal this mystery of friendship hidden in our Lord's heart by the example of our lives or by mentioning it to a few friends only?

From the point of view of a contemplative vocation a reserve of this kind can be justified by two reasons: in the first place, it discloses one aspect of God's love, and imitates it; secondly, it is often an indispensable practice if the word of God is to find an entry into men's souls. The first belongs to the realm of contemplation, it is a kind of reflection of God's own existence as the lover of mankind. The second belongs rather to the realm of apostolic charity, which must organise its activities so that its message may reach all men. Both these reasons are closely interdependent.

The conversion of men's minds to the faith and of their hearts to the embrace of Christ's love is the goal of the apostolate, which sets the whole process moving to its attainment. The obvious purpose of the various methods of transmission and preaching it employs is to effect conversion and initiate belief.

The Petits Frères' vocation, on the other hand, is to make our Lord known and loved without using any of the means that directly aim at conversion. This is not to deny that they must wholeheartedly desire the conversion of those they love. They could not possibly do otherwise. Their desire is as great, as important and ambitious as that of the most active apostle. If, indeed, they were not utterly absorbed by it, their love would not be either genuine or open-handed, and their friendship, now purely human, would be limited to an intercourse from which God was excluded. But what they intend, what God seems to have indicated as their vocation, is to exhibit, through the way they love, that mysterious respect for the minds and hearts of created beings which we find in God. This unwearying patience of the divine mercy stands humbly at the door of the sinner and the unbeliever, stands and waits. God's action is irresistible, and yet he also seems to wait.

The father of the prodigal son was transported by love as his own son drew near, and showed himself to him—thereby scandalising the loyalists at home—even before he knew whether this lad he was embracing had repented, even before the boy had knelt appealingly before him. God's love is so overwhelmingly urgent that it must have this silence, patience, and apparent unconcern, in order to make itself manifest and prove to a doubter that he is loved for his own sake.

So long as a man has not received the light of faith, so long as he does not know that one absolute Truth exists, the initiative of a friend openly trying to convince him will be suspect. But if a man can be offered an entirely disinterested friendship in which he will be loved for his own sake, and if at the same time no attempt is made to convince him of the faith or guide him to it—without of course concealing our own belief —then this may be the one way of enabling him to realise the fullness of love which is in God . . .

Do not say that this is simply a technique, a cunning method employed to cover up the real aim, which is conversion. This would be true only if an apostle's motive was not that of genuine love, and it would then prove to be a singularly defective method! But if it really is what it ought to be, this discreet silence will be both completely genuine and completely loyal to one's friend, inasmuch as it accords with the way God himself would act. This is why we said above that the two reasons justifying our silent testimony are closely connected: authentic love is always in harmony with that which is divinely true.

In this way, therefore, we are expressing one real aspect of God's love. The need to bear witness to it is all the greater because the active apostolate is not always sufficiently inspired by such disinterested charity. We know how difficult it is for an apostle to avoid self-seeking . . . The struggle to make others share our own beliefs can have an ominous attraction! The various activities undertaken to achieve this end by propaganda, are sometimes *outwardly* very similar to those of an authentic apostolate. In every day usage, the word 'apostle' is equally applied to a doctor, a communist, a socialist, a theosophist so convinced of the truth of his own ideas that he will devote his life to spreading them. Christian and missionary apostolic action may therefore seem to unbelievers to have an uncommon likeness to techniques of this kind. Silent witness would thus seem to supply an essential complement to the Church's apostolate.

If that apostolate is to be truly Christ's it will make certain definite demands; and in its turn the witness of silence makes its own demands. But this testimony given by our lives cannot always exclude the testimony of the word; there are occasions when the latter becomes a strict duty which we owe to truth or love. A systematic refusal to speak of God, or even, in certain cases, to teach the faith or proclaim the gospel, when such a ministry is requested by those whom providence has guided to our door, would be incompatible with the claims of Christian truth. Even so, the Petits Frères must keep clear of any attempt to proselytise, any organised use of methods of persuasion or of transmission of the faith, and as a general rule must refuse to accept the responsibility for any official ministry of preaching. If they did accept it this would involve disloyalty to their vocation, which obliges them to remain in the reserved and respectful waiting proper to friendship.

A repeated failure to maintain this reserve would mean that the Brotherhoods were disabling themselves from carrying out their mission to those countless people who can only discover the Church and come to know Christ through a friendship which involves no proselytism. How would it be possible to go on living on friendly terms with Mohammedans, Protestants, atheists, or Marxists who have only accepted us because we said we would not proselytise, if they should find that, in fact, we are breaking this promise?

In order that such an attitude may not be a mere technique for making contact with people, it must be lived out as a genuine reproduction of the love which springs from the heart of Christ, a reproduction which contemplative prayer can alone make possible.

I realise the problems that arise from the apparently contradictory demands made by a completely loyal adherence to the truth encountered in faith, on the one hand, and the equally loyal adherence to a disinterested but too human friendship, on the other. How simple it would be if we could keep our desire that our friends should believe in Christ locked away in our hearts, without expressing it outwardly. A Mohammedan, a Protestant, or an unbelieving friend will always be glad when he finds that our friendship involves no unsettling of his own convictions. His idea of loyalty and disinterestedness in friendship may in fact lead him to exact complete neutrality. After all, we *have* asserted that the purpose of our presence is simply to provide a witness to our friendship, that no overtones of proselytism shall accompany it, and this assertion has been accepted. If we bear witness to the son of God and to revealed truth, should we be betraying this trust? This is one of the most difficult issues that a Petit Frère has to face. How can he reconcile the rights of truth with those of hospitality and loyal friendship?

He must learn the way to wait quietly for God's hour to strike, and so take his part in the infinite patience of divine providence. In the development of each of our friendships there comes a moment, a point fixed by God, when witness to the truth of the son of God must be expressed in words, however discreetly. Sometimes the absolute frankness and honesty of our friendship acts as a more powerful incentive to accept Christian truth than many of the activities directly aimed at conversion. At times truth may demand great courage. To keep faith unwaveringly with both God and man is a task of considerable difficulty. We must not sacrifice any element of the truth, nor pretend that a given situation is simpler than in fact it is. If the Petits Frères fail to keep their attention firmly fixed on God, and do not base themselves solidly on the assistance of our Lord's spirit, they will find their task impossible.

The temptation to sacrifice the intellectual consequences of adhering to revealed truth in order to maintain the unity achieved by love is not an illusory danger. Some may well be drawn to take this easier road because it seems the quicker way to the haven of united hearts. But a contemplative is bound to suffer deeply at the sight of truth unacknowledged or rejected. Even where there is no question of conversion, circumstances are bound to crop up that make it necessary for a Petit Frère to give his testimony to the truth. Loyalty to the true Church or to the Christian faith may sometimes compel him, as it were in spite of himself, to accept the break up of a friendship, or at least its diminution. Our Lord was and will remain until the end of time a sign of contradiction among men, even among those who are intimate friends, and he foretold that this would be so even in the most united families.

The only reason for our way of life is to love Christ and to ensure that he is loved. This truth cannot be brushed aside. For our presence among others in friendship is not our ultimate purpose. Any brother who remains satisfied with this either through passivity or lack of faith, will soon become heart-sick. Life, as it develops, is never simple. To the extent in which the brethren have given their complete friendship to a people who do not share their faith, they will, sooner or later, find themselves confronted by problems concerning the spread of the gospel, or to do with the assistance needed for projects in the social, economic, or educational spheres.

It may happen, in fact, that those to whom a Brotherhood has been sent are ready to receive instruction or even ask for it. This is an eventuality which, sometime or other, may be expected to occur.

Can it be said that the initiation of people into the Christian faith is a work that is no concern of ours. Have we any right to hold this view? Shall we stay silent, refusing the testimony of the word, making the 'division of labour', and the fact that it is not our vocation, our excuse? Like a worker who has finished his job and does not bother about the person coming on the next shift.

In 1911 Father de Foucauld was envisaging just such an eventuality when he wrote:

According to aptitudes, attractions and needs, and the Superior's estimate of God's will, every group of three or four religious will devote each of its members either completely to manual labour, or partly to manual labour and

156

partly to apostolic work, or almost entirely to apostolic work. The apostolic work that I have practised up to the present, and as I now envisage it, consists of individual conversations with unbelievers (and when the need arises, with Christians) . . . There might, however, be more extensive instruction to be given and the initial stages of a ministry established. I view these outposts as forerunners preparing the way who will hand over to other religious, organised on the lines of the secular clergy, once the ground has been cleared.

This passage is quite definite. He sees what may be called two kinds of apostolic activity in which the Brotherhoods will be engaged: the first forms part of the normal life of a Brotherhood and consists of individual contacts in chance conversations during which a Petit Frère, while respecting the obligations of friendship, must bear witness by words, that is, by teaching the faith. The other, more exceptional, is described by Father de Foucauld as the initial stages of the ministry to be begun while awaiting the arrival of other religious, 'organised on the lines of the secular clergy'. It is, however, certain that the dividing line between the preparatory work which is the normal duty of the Petit Frère and the assumption of responsibility for the ministry which is the work of priests or religious, is often difficult to decide in an absolutely definite way. The 'initial stages of the ministry' may be guaranteed by the Petits Frères acting as a temporary substitute. After all, is not the achievement of this result the reason why every Petit Frère is sent? Is not the long-term preparation for the time when their unbelieving friends will approach the Church the mission of every individual brother, and do not those of them who are priests fulfil their priesthood in this way? It is with the joy of a mission accomplished that a Brotherhood must respond to the initial demands made by evangelisation and the ministry.

It is easy enough to say that a Brotherhood must stop at the threshold of a real pastoral ministry in the name of the Church . . . and yet in practice it is very difficult to define the boundary beyond which apostolic work must be entrusted to other religious or priests 'organised on the lines of the secular clergy'.

The Petits Frères are therefore called to prepare the way for the direct preaching of the gospel and the establishment of the Church. This is why, for preference, they will go to those who are farthest from the Church. It follows that in principle their vocation does not call them to practise their apostolate within a Christian society, and they must not abandon a difficult sector of the apostolate for another better prepared to receive the faith, where the needs are certainly urgent, but to which they had not been assigned. The prospect of more extensive and immediate results might induce a belief in a duty of charity which does not in fact exist.

On the other hand, it is natural that after a Brotherhood has been present in an unbelieving environment for some years, it should be led to take provisional charge of the beginning of a ministry in a Christian community in its formative stage, and which they have helped to create. A more delicate problem arises when a Brotherhood is established in a region in which unbelievers or de-christianised people are existing side by side with a Christian community. The Petits Frères who are priests will find themselves faced with a situation that may well be baffling, because Christians will expect them to minister to their needs. It would, at any rate, be wrong to assert too readily that a Brotherhood ought not to be established in such regions where a Christian community is being steadily de-christianised and where its witness may be absolutely essential.

The way in which a Petit Frère may be moved to solve the cases of conscience which he has to face will vary according to his temperament and the personal circumstances of his vocation. Even so, he will be obliged to take his cue, more or less, from the following principles.

A Petit Frère who is a priest is primarily committed to bear witness to the gospel among those who are outside the Church. This is the reason for his ordination to proclaim the gospel, even if those for whom he has been hallowed have not yet asked for the sacraments. But the example of his poverty and toil and the influence of the spirituality which propels him, will attract laymen or priests who will ask him to practise his ministry or preach. We may deceive ourselves if we jump to the conclusion that we have an obligation in charity to meet these requests. This is especially true when the proposed ministry would separate a Petit Frère from those who have either given up the practise of their religion or are hostile to the Church and need his silent friendship and apparently functionless priesthood if they are to recover their belief in God. It is here that the deception may lie.

The local clergy with a Christian community in their care who see the function of a priest primarily from the point of view of the administration of the sacraments and direct instruction, will probably fail to understand this friendship expressed simply by being present among non-Christians with no apparently useful purpose. And yet it does not seem to be a Petit Frère's duty—apart from exceptional circumstances that would not entail the abandonment of his state of life—to meet such requests for his ministry, even though there may be a scarcity of priests in the region. For if priests were under a permanent obligation of this kind, would it not be the duty for Carthusians to leave their cells, bishops' secretaries their offices, and ecclesiastical professors their teaching posts? The only situation which might give rise to a case of conscience for a Petit Frère and make him ask whether he is really fulfilling his calling, would be that of a Brotherhood whose toil and silent testimony of prayer lacked all apostolic utility because no part of the region was so de-christianised

159

that it needed this kind of existential apostolate. In this case a Petit Frère will feel that he must go and plant himself elsewhere, in some place where our Lord is not acknowledged and men are unconsciously waiting for his testimony of silent friendship and prayer.

6

The Place of Poverty
in Apostolic Action

Unlike the previous chapters which were mainly concerned
with the Petits Frères, the following notes have been written
with the aim of being of some assistance . . . to all priests and
lay people engaged in the ministry or the apostolate. [I
hope] that they will enable them to see more easily how the
example of Brother Charles of Jesus may be a guide for them,
even though he himself lived as a priest entirely alone and
uniquely devoted to the work of missionary preparation
connected with the life of Nazareth.

Every aspect of the apostolate—that of the hierarchy or,
more broadly, that of the Christian community—finds its
outlet in a number of activities which, however, all originate
in the faith and love dwelling in an apostle's heart. In the
Church there are many kinds of apostolate; some are called
by God to initiate activities of great power in Christ's service;
others are called to employ slender means and to an apostolic
life which at least looks less effective. But all of them have
a common share in our Lord's apostolate and all of them are
equally needed by the Church. Every apostle is thus led to
inquire what means he will need for the exercise of his
apostolate and what principles must guide his selection from
these infinitely varied activities, all of which are more or less
suitable for enabling the unique message of our Lord to

F

reach all men in their different historical epochs and civilisations.

An apostle's sole desire must be to make our Lord, the son of God, known and loved, whatever the means he or providence may choose. St. Paul gives us a striking example of this:

I want you to know, brethren, that what has happened to me, has really served to advance the gospel, so that it has become known throughout the whole praetorian guard and to all the rest, that my imprisonment is for Christ, and most of the brethren have been made confident in the Lord because of my imprisonment, and are much more bold to speak the word of God without fear. Some indeed preach Christ from envy and rivalry, but others from good will . . . What then? Only that in every way, whether in pretence or in truth, Christ is proclaimed; and in that I rejoice. (Phil. 1:12–18.)

The means employed are of little account, provided they are legitimate and that Christ is proclaimed. Love cannot do otherwise than wish that the apostolate may succeed. Our Lord deeply desired the salvation of his brethren and the coming of his Father's kingdom; and we in turn can wish for nothing else. Therefore we may not, on account of our personal calling to practise poverty or the humiliation of the cross, implicitly wish for a diminution in our apostolic activities. For this would also mean that we would be content to see our Lord less widely known and some of our brethren failing to benefit from the fullness of grace to be found in the Church.

When he entrusted the preaching of the Kingdom to men, our Lord thereby linked the apostolate with the use of human means of teaching, transmitting, and convincing. The organisation of the Church as a human society, an organisation conceived and intended by Christ himself, is completed by the bestowal of the attribute of a human social activity upon the apostolate. Our choice, therefore, lies between apostolic activities of great diversity.

How is this choice to be made? It is not enough to decide by the light of reason alone on the most propitious means for the success of the apostolate. Besides, in practice it is very difficult to define what, in the apostolate, must be considered a success! For, under its human trappings, the apostolate remains a personal activity of Christ in his Body the Church, an activity as mysterious as the person of the Word incarnate. The Church's life flows right through into all her apostolic work.

The difficulty in this sphere of action arises from the fact that a man finds it hard to form a judgement about his own activities according to a criterion that is beyond reason. He finds it difficult to admit the mystery at work within his own personal deeds. For the apostolate is supernatural not only in the truths it puts forward, or in the apostle's heart enlightened through the contemplation of the mysteries of God and inspired by divine love; it is also supernatural *in what it does*. Apostolic action, therefore, cannot be separated from the mysterious union between the human and the divine which marks the mystery of the incarnation, nor from the evangelical principles which it is its mission to transmit.

This is the precise problem which faces every apostle whatever the nature of his apostolate, be it the ministry of the priesthood, or Christian witness, missionary activity, or Catholic Action.

To what extent must the Beatitudes affect the way an apostle acts, so as to transform this into an expression of the directives in the gospel to use 'poor' means? For when we have discussed the adaptation of means to the mentality of the environment or to the temperament of the apostle, much still remains to be said. God also has his word to say with regard to an action which in a sense he makes his own, and which he must be able to use as an instrument for the manifestation of his glory and for the creation of divine faith in souls.

We ought to be clear at once that it is lawful to use the most technically adapted and powerful means for the purposes of the apostolate, and that these have an aptitude to produce an effect that is truly supernatural. To deny this would be to run counter to the directives and encouragement given by the Church on a number of occasions. When they have been made the servants of authentic love and employed in a spirit of poverty, these means have contributed greatly to the Church's apostolate.

The problem, however, is not quite so simple. The history of the Church often shows us that the most profound and lasting spiritual results have issued from the employment of 'poor' means, means whose intrinsic nature is disproportionate to the scope of the results obtained.

The content of the message to be transmitted must also be kept in mind. For it is not a mere moral code corresponding to a restricted and natural human destiny. The redemption operates in such a way that the great commandment of fraternal love is practicable only in the spirit of the Sermon on the Mount. Only our Lord could have really propounded the seven beatitudes as good news. For this latter is based upon a twofold reality: on the one hand, there is the brute fact that among men, poverty, suffering, weakness, and violence exist; and on the other, the declaration that all these things . . . will henceforth be transformed for men, through our Lord's death and resurrection, into means of achieving redemption, of bringing in God's reign and the establishment of peace.

Is not Christ's work essentially the transformation of human infirmities into instruments that are productive of divine life and eternal beatitude? And must not the means used in order to transmit this message be also themselves conformed to the news transmitted? Is there not a danger that the mode of transmission may distort it, or, more simply, prevent the apostle from delivering it in its integrity? Can the blessedness of poverty be proclaimed to men through means which depends upon wealth? Or the kingdom of the meek and the peacemakers by taking advantage of a position of prestige? Or the blessedness of those who mourn, when we deliberately choose a sheltered life, on the pretext that life needs to be organised if it is to produce a better apostolic return?

At the same time it is true that the passionate eagerness of the messenger whom love has made impatient, will drive him to use the most effective means, and in doing so he will be in conformity with many of the Church's recommendations. Once again we must accept the antimonies that follow from the incarnation and the mystery of the Church. It is not our business to pronounce a ban on either term of the alternatives; we have to make a choice, personal to each of us, that is relative to our vocation and to the demands made by preaching the gospel in a given set of circumstances.

It will, of course, be said that [the employment of elaborate modern techniques] is entirely for the sake of serving the truth. But the question that matters is whether the apostle is also wholeheartedly serving the son of God and his gospel. The more technically developed a means becomes, the more an activity is powerfully organised, the greater the danger that the apostle's spirit will be affected and influenced by the very means he uses. The activity which ought to be only the opportunity or the instrument of the apostolate becomes the sole reason for action and existence on the part of a man who believes that he is still an apostle, whereas he may be one no longer. It is a matter of extreme difficulty. For in spite of his mission, an apostle is only a man like other men, subject to the same temptations and infirmities.

Human wealth on earth is not made up solely of bank accounts or real estate; the will to power, the passion for action, politics, journalism, the trade-union struggle, or the practice of medicine, can all monopolise the human mind and heart, in the same way as what is commonly called wealth. It is in this sense that we can speak of the wealth of certain means of action. Does the head of a mission who administers schools, institutions of every kind, who is responsible for a number of buildings and occasionally directly running a business, escape the temptations that a layman with similar responsibilities encounters in the world, simply from the fact that his work is at the service of the mission? The position of an apostle who is obliged to use these means is like that of a rich man not actually called to surrender his wealth, but to administer it in a spirit of poverty. So when such activities are adopted and employed, the essential thing is to remain true to the evangelical counsels: 'Truly, I say to you, it will be hard for a rich man to enter the kingdom of heaven. Again I tell you, it is easier for a camel to go through the eye of a needle than for a rich man to enter the kingdom of God' (Matt. 19:23–4).

The heart of a priest, a religious, or a lay apostle is not sheltered from temptations of this kind simply because his activities are sincerely intended to serve the Church. In these matters illusion can insinuate itself with great subtlety, and Christ's imperatives remain absolute. To retain poverty of spirit, convinced that the apostolate transcends the means employed, to know how to sustain the involuntary loss of these means with tranquillity, to preserve a humble and un-assuming heart before God and man when we find ourselves in positions that bestow power to control other people— these are the indispensable dispositions of an apostle of our Lord. He must try to maintain them amidst the fever of activity and the exalted satisfaction which every success pro-duces.

Apostolic means that are 'poor' are always simple, and most often consist of returning to essentials, that is, to the most direct apostolic action possible, such as the testimony given by our lives, by preaching and divine worship, indirect action being given up. When the apostolate is undertaken in this way, it must not only correspond with a personal vocation but also be in conformity with the needs of the environment to be evangelised. It is perhaps more difficult to decide on the use of 'poor' means than it is to employ those that are normal for a given situation, because the former largely depend upon the unforeseeable action of divine grace and the supernatural preparation of the apostle.

Those who are called to give up burdensome or over-elaborate technical means that aim at extending the diffusion of our Lord's message, securing opportunities for contact, or at gaining an influence over men's minds, will sometimes have to accept a narrowed sphere of activity as a consequence. This may well lead to fewer results, but it may be compensated by a supernatural penetration due to the omnipotent action of Christ's grace . . .

The call to devote one's life to the apostolate using only 'poor' means in no way implies that the search for results has been abandoned, any more than when our Lord withdrew into the wilderness, and refused to hasten the coming of God's kingdom by producing signs that startle, he abandoned his intention that it should, in fact, succeed.

Some, indeed, may be tempted to turn a kind of flight from action into an ideal, either through timidity, or through attachment to a smooth-running life, or simply because they are afraid of making an effort. This is not what is under discussion here! For the gospel prescribes violence in the renunciations we are to make: 'The kingdom of heaven has suffered violence, and men of violence take it by storm' (Matt. 11:12). 'For whoever would save his life will lose it, and whoever loses his life for my sake will find it' (Matt. 16:25).

For if this adoption of 'poor' means is to be in conformity with the gospel, it presupposes the conviction that they are supremely effective. This conviction springs from faith. It also depends on the idea we have formed of what 'success' in the apostolate really means. How difficult it is to estimate the value of such realities as the guidance of men to believe in the son of God, to live in conformity with the gospel, to worship in spirit and in truth, to dwell together in fraternal love, by the standard of some external result! Who would be sufficiently presumptuous to claim that he could measure the degree of progress which God's kingdom has made in men's souls?

Asceticism in action . . . ranks equally with the employ-ment of other means. The absence of organised activity is in no way a sign that the dynamism of love has slackened. Nevertheless, this poverty in action must be the consequence of authentic inner qualities—love, prayer, humility, simplicity. The apostolate carried out through the use of 'poor' means is like the continuation in outward activity of a personal life devoted to putting our Lord's counsels into practice.

Since the natural power of such activity is out of all proportion with its ultimate result—the conversion of men's hearts—it allows the power of grace to be made manifest in that result. In this way God chooses to show the wealth of his grace through the humbling of human pride and its will to power, for the glory of his love alone . . .

This is what Brother Charles of Jesus was trying to express when he wrote: 'the weakness of the means employed by man is a cause of strength'. No doubt; but on one condition: the weakness of the human means must be the result of a real union with Christ, poor, humble, and crucified, so that the strength of his grace can use this weakness as an instrument of supernatural power. We must not deceive ourselves: an apostolate based on the means indicated in the gospel is in-conceivable unless the apostle has been totally penetrated by the spirit and counsels of the gospel. Such means cease to produce results if they are severed from a heart in union with Christ. The other means, however, may continue to deceive, for they will still possess a natural power of their own, but its relationship to the Church's divine life is in appearance only. 'Poor' means, on the other hand, if severed from the context of an integrally Christian life, become completely useless. They do not preserve even the appearance of being effective, for they possess no intrinsic power. The purpose of their nature is to present an unoccupied area which leaves room for the divine action to enter and become visible. Considered in their relationship with the apostolate and the prophetic office, the means laid down in the gospel are a necessary expression of the divine nature of the Church and of our Lord's all-powerful action within his mystical body.

PART THREE

Extracts from a Diary, 1950–60

1950

I have received a letter from a brother which moves me to speak to you briefly about 'worldwide love'. I quote his words: 'What worries me personally is my inability to love the poor with the same intensity as my brethren do. I love all men, but particularly the rich because they seem to me to be farther away from God. The poor, on the other hand, are so close to him that they cannot be counted as the most disinherited. Therefore, it is not on their account that I love material poverty in life, but because Jesus himself owned nothing, and because, as St. Augustine says, it leads one progressively to become content with as little as possible.'

In my view, this brother has no need to worry, because the more intimately we are united with our Lord, the more universal our love becomes. In God's sight all men are naked and stripped, the rich of their riches, and the poor of the little they possess. Our Lord loves *man*, and he is not greatly concerned with man's social context. Poverty and riches are relevant only to the extent in which they affect the soul, either liberating or enslaving it. This deliverance or these bonds are situated in the depths of the human heart, and it is this that our Lord sees, and for this reason he commiserates the rich and blesses the poor, although he loves both equally. He cursed riches, but not the rich. His curse was directed to the hypocrisy, pride, and hardness of heart, which wealth often produces.

We must have a special love for the poor because they are usually despised by other men, because their wretchedness weighs on them like a garment which repels, and makes them ignored and spurned. It may be this that accounts for their being nearer to God than the rich. It also explains why love for them is sure to be largely free from human motivation and is directed in a singular way to our Lord. Instinctively, we all feel tempted to turn away from a poor and wretched man, and this explains why we are bound to give him a quite exceptional love. Nevertheless, we should be acting in opposition to the desires of God's heart if we allowed ourselves to entertain the slightest contempt for the rich, the least withdrawal of our love for them. For they also are in their own way poor and wretched. When our hearts have expanded into a universal love for all men, whether they are poor or rich, without respect of persons, when we pay no more attention to the rich on account of their wealth or to the poor on account of their wretchedness, we are beginning to love men as Jesus loved them.

We should realise that some brothers feel especially drawn to the poor and that love is approached by many different paths. As a community, the Brotherhood embraces all men with a worldwide love. Father de Foucauld repeated this over and over again. And yet this universality . . . does not exclude our obligation to establish our Brotherhoods among the poor, and our choice of them in preference to the rich.

Father de Foucauld wrote: 'We shall, of course, have a brotherly interest in the wealthy, but really these have friends in plenty who are eager to see that they have a comfortable life! They are our Lord's healthy members; the poor are his members who are sick and bleeding. We shall honour them all equally, but we shall bind up the wounds of the poor before we contribute delicacies to those in good health.'

Our approach to those whom fortune has favoured will

most often be that of an example of brotherly love towards the poor and the working classes. Experience overwhelmingly convinces us that members of the possessing classes are never without need of instruction on this subject.

El-Abiodh-Sidi-Cheikh, 9 March

1951

It is very difficult to find a title for a book that is short, concrete, and that also expresses an essential characteristic of the Brotherhoods. Out of all the possible titles that occurred to me, 'At the heart of the Masses',[1] seems much the best, although by no means perfect. It is, of course, open to criticism; the perfect title does not exist. But I believe that it is a reasonably good expression of one of the characteristic aspects of our way of life; that aspect which impels us towards the poorest of mankind, towards that utter poverty of the masses who are ruled by false shepherds or by ideologies that degrade the dignity of the human person.

However much of a cliché the word 'masses' may have become, we cannot find any other that expresses the twentieth-century phenomenon of the extinction of human individuality by materialism. It is not to be understood as signifying a contrast with an élite, but in its obvious meaning. In this sense we can speak of Chinese, Mohammedan, and Black masses, that after being delivered from domination by the West will now be no less crushed by a technical civilisation that will increase their dehumanisation under the guise of material prosperity. Need I mention the European working classes, the 'displaced persons', and the anonymous multitude? It is to these people that we have been sent as carriers of a brotherly message of friendship from our saviour, Christ. We cannot remain apart from them, nor can we just settle on their frontiers; we must

[1] *Au Cœur des Masses* (*Seeds of the Desert*, op. cit.).

penetrate right into their heart. The way *they* live must influence the way *we* live, must give the outward form of our religious life its specific character. This is what I tried to indicate by the title: *Au Cœur des Masses*.

Zinder (Nigeria), 2 January

This new foundation [in the midst of two primitive tribes in the mountains of the North Cameroons], must keep intact the spirit of Father de Foucauld and pave the way for others. It will have to adapt itself to an entirely new environment that presents very special problems of its own. These problems arise from its isolation, its scarcity of material necessities, its oppressive climate, its people entirely outside your experience, its languages, which at least as regards the Ouldemes and the Madas you have been the first to interpret.

I will begin with the most important and basic factor: the message of brotherly love which all missionaries and the Brotherhoods in particular are bound to convey. This message meets peculiar difficulties in these circumstances. We are Europeans, and our African brothers may not yet know us as we really are. Those around us in the mountains of Mora have hardly ever seen a European.

Our technical civilisation with its complicated material requirements (witness our own encampment), together with the needs of Western man condemned to an exhausting climate, means that there is a level below which we may not go. As a result of this, the approach of these simple people, who have no artificial needs, to the simplicity of the gospel message as perceptible in us, is made most difficult. And yet we are the only bearers of this message to them.

They differ so much from us that we are always on the point of misunderstanding them and making false judgements about them. Precisely because we are what we are there is a danger that we may import many things which not only do not belong to the gospel, or to the unalloyed Christian message, but are also harmful or degrading. Very often we can do nothing about it, and this should be a source of grief.

This fact supplies an additional reason for us to return again and again to the reality of a genuine brotherhood. These people may seem remote from us, and difficult at times to understand, but we must go on loving them with infinite respect. We are their brothers in Christ's name, and it is unnecessary to repeat that our mission in its entirety is concerned with loving and understanding them, after the fashion of our Lord.

This is not idealism, it is the concrete reality of the mission entrusted to us by the Church. We shall constantly be tempted to take a different view because our relationship with them is bound to be on the level of material collaboration. Without realising it, we look at them from a European point of view, and criticise them from a Western standpoint. No doubt we love them, but perhaps somewhat condescendingly, introducing a note of pity, and fail to give them the respect that is their due. Our ideas of punctuality, of a regular output of work, of social relationships, do not seem to them to possess universal validity for every human being.

I am thinking particularly of the primitive people of the North Cameroons. To you they will seem like children. This is untrue, but it is how you will treat them! When they are confronted by some of the material aspects of a civilisation that is entirely new to them, you may think their reactions childish and that you must treat them as children. But you will be wrong. They are in no degree less human and adult than ourselves, human in every sense of the word, greatly human in their triumph over stark conditions of life, in their pride and independence, in the struggle for existence which their arid mountains inflict upon them. The total absence of needs which we consider to be essential is no intrinsic indication of inferiority, especially in the eyes of our Lord who penetrates to the heart of every man.

You cannot hope to know what takes place between God and the souls of these men, your whole energy must be devoted to trying to understand, love, and respect them, as our Lord would have done had he lived among them.

In the name of our Lord's love, I beg you not to criticise them, never make fun of them, never be witty at their expense. Jesus would not, could not, have done so. A mother or a father would not behave in this way towards their children. Condemn moral evil, but nothing else. Never condemn lack of experience, lack of adaptation to some particular form of work; you will certainly need help, and you must work with them. They will not know what to do, they may be clumsy and negligent, they may break or damage utensils you entrust them with, they may spoil a job you have given them. Remember that there may be nothing morally wrong in any of this. Do not judge, do not condemn, never laugh at them because of such mistakes. Of course, some expressions of impatience will be inevitable; you must do your best; God will understand. But I implore you, do not coldly cast a judgement of inferiority upon them, do not emphasise their errors, however real these may be, never mock them. Remember that for them you are the bearers of Christ's love, that for them you are Christ actually present.

Think of the centuries of intellectual culture that have been needed to produce a mentality such as ours. These people are not unintelligent simply because they take time to understand our explanations; their minds are unaccustomed to functioning in a culture shaped like ours, that is all. We are far too Cartesian, and our civilisation is materially so overdeveloped that we dare not claim to be unequivocally human in our judgements.

It is a danger from which we cannot hope permanently to escape. A colonist, a leading industrialist, a teacher, an administrator will judge them from the criterion of the stage they have reached in material development. This may be legitimate, and in any case is inevitable. It is a tragedy due to the confrontation of two peoples divided by centuries of historical evolution. But the missionary, the messenger of the gospel, has no right to take this standpoint; you will be tempted to take it, however, just in so far as you have to work among them.

Petits Frères, I implore you, even though you may not understand them, and precisely *because* you may not understand them, love them as brothers, with respect and humility. Seek out the true qualities of their race and emphasise them. Some of these are splendid, and you will learn their value. With them as a foundation, that kind of Christianity and holy living will be developed which God means them to attain, and will reach its specific perfection.

Douala, 16 February

I am increasingly certain that our form of poverty must be that of poor workmen, ordinary craftsmen, smallholders who have to earn their living, and I am sure that this must be the Brotherhoods' way of life. I think it is correct to say that so far we have been true to this aspect of our vocation; most of the Brotherhoods have lived in poverty, with no security, no help from outside, and have often had to work extremely hard. Many have had to endure more or less lengthy periods of deprivation, and all have loyally shared the circumstances of the lives of those with whom they have worked.

But I am also increasingly certain that our novices need formation, need a serious study of theology and languages. And further, I am sure that we must not hesitate to answer a call from a distant people even if it costs money to reach them. Such things need a budget which cannot at once be met simply by the work of the brethren. And yet, are not such formative requirements and such distant foundations direct consequences of the missionary vocation entrusted to us by the Church?

If for the time being we refused to accept other resources, this would immediately involve the suppression of remote brotherhoods, make the theological and linguistic training of the brethren impossible and frustrate many vocations. The apostolic zeal of Brother Charles of Jesus would have exploded in a vessel too constricted to contain it. An attitude of this kind would mean that love would have to be confined within the limits of material poverty uniformly based on what work can produce, whereas truth demands that the poverty of a disciple of our Lord shall be subordinated to the commands of love and zeal. 'In order that the gospel may be transmitted, I am ready to go to the ends of the earth . . .'

In the footsteps of Brother Charles, we have chosen to *imitate the poverty of the worker of Nazareth* and through love to share the lot of the poor. Hence every brotherhood must staunchly maintain a way of life that enables us, with no thought of self, to follow our Lord's counsels joyfully and thus become the brothers and friends of the poor. This means, we repeat, sharing their lot lovingly with a view to bringing Christ to them in his Church. It is a mission that no one can take from us, and we have no right to give up whatever may be necessary to carry it out.

'To be a worker like other workers,' however, is not an end in itself. The end is defined by the drive to give God to others. Therefore you cannot agree to become in every respect a worker like other workers. You may not, for instance, accept a lodging so impoverished that there is no room for a simple oratory where you can pray to our Lord, you have no right to take up systematic work of a kind that will make your vocation to Christian living and prayer impossible. You have no right to give up the elementary conditions of life that are essential if you are to develop your faith—a development in the truth that is necessary not only for yourselves personally, but in order that you may become the light of the world.

How can the acceptance of a state of poverty, of which the

only guiding light is absolute conformity with every aspect of the life of the poor, be justified? I agree that in so far as it is not essentially incompatible with your vocation as Christians, apostles, and men of prayer, it can be. But because those around us accept conditions that are incompatible with a minimum of spiritual or even properly human life, are you bound to accept them solely on the grounds that your vocation allows you to have nothing that the poorest labourer is unable to possess?

The answer is, again, yes—in so far as Christ urges and commands us to do so. But pay attention to Brother Charles of Jesus, be poor in the way he was, with the boundless zeal of an utterly loving heart. I would rather hear you say that your poverty is modelled on that of Jesus of Nazareth than on the way of life of the workers around you, and I ask you to believe that my emphasis on this is due simply to my desire to see that you always keep material poverty subordinate to charity and to our mission in the Church.

You may perhaps reply: We agree, but is it not a fact that our mission in the Church is precisely that of disappearing among the poor and renouncing every method of apostolising incompatible with that state of poverty? Was it not in order to safeguard this vocation that Brother Charles of Jesus himself refused, and formally insisted that his brethren should refuse, to undertake any organised activity or mission? This is indeed true, but there are two things he never renounced and to which he subordinated the poverty of his brethren: he never renounced the requirements that are indispensable for the development of a life of prayer and of union with Christ, nor did he ever renounce what he needed in order that he could live among men and understand them, with the aim of bringing them the testimony of the gospel. Neither can *we* renounce these things; but we must do our utmost to reconcile the demands they make with those of poverty.

Father de Foucauld foresaw the need for the establishment

of Brotherhoods in Christian countries 'in order to obtain the resources necessary for the Brotherhoods in the mission field'. He was well aware that if a response was to be made to an appeal from some distant and helpless people, money would be needed. Can you imagine that we could turn a deaf ear and harden our hearts, when a wordless appeal reaches us from some section of suffering humanity, or from those deprived of the light of the gospel? Ought we to give a negative reply because a foundation of this kind would involve a transfer beyond the resources of an ordinary workman? Carthusians can refuse to establish themselves in a country where the observance of their rule would be impossible, because their vocation is not bound up with the needs of any particular locality. But we cannot take this line, since contact with men and incorporation in their lives is an essential element in our vocation.

In each case we must see to it that the essential conditions are established for living as a Brotherhood that is genuinely poor. But we must also be most careful not to allow the idea of the poverty God wants from us to become too rigid and be reduced to that of 'working for a living'. That may conceal not only something of the pride of a man who wants to rely for his resources upon himself alone, but also a refusal to accept either the uncertainty of tomorrow or the humiliation of having to receive help from other people.

Of course, the criterion of living poorly must be adapted to the mentality of each age in turn; in our time, therefore, the comparative poverty of the ordinary wage earner, or of the unskilled manual worker is especially relevant ... Is it not our mission to help to make the Church and the religious life present in the midst of these proletarian masses whose lot we mean to share? But this adaptation cannot extend to the sacrifice of essential values. How often we have heard this or that way of life condemned simply because it would not be understood, because it would shock or scandalise or repel.

The discussion raises the whole problem of adaptation; in principle, it seems clear enough, but its application to concrete situations raises many difficulties. We realise that anything accidental may be altered, and that it is a duty to do everything in our power to make ourselves understood, but when it is a question of a Christian or evangelical truth we may not suppress or even modify it without denying our mission as witnesses of the gospel. Our Lord himself did not act in a way that would be understood by everybody, although in his method of teaching and in his actions, he always tried to avoid giving needless offence. But with regard to the essentials of his message, he was intransigent. He did not fear to offend, nor did he stop when he was misunderstood; and it cost him his life.

To wish to say and do nothing that cannot be understood is tempting and seems like an easy solution to all difficulties. It is a temptation common enough today, and is the counterpart of an authentic attempt to achieve religious renewal and realism. It is particularly subtle because we find it most distasteful not to be understood; human respect makes us dread a shrug of the shoulders or sarcasm. Can you believe that in a materialistic environment whose only idea of progress is that of a human civilisation organised with ever-increasing rationality, the Christian message, imbued with God's mystery and transcendence, will be understood, let alone accepted? Is it possible for the Church, whose visible organisation is involved in this mysterious and sometimes paradoxical reality, to avoid being misunderstood?

Our mission is intimately connected with the Church. Are we to give it up simply because it is not understood by workers infected with a Marxist mentality or by some reputed Christians who have lost all sense of the Church? It will very often prove to be impossible to avoid imparting a shock or even giving scandal.

An ordinary worker obviously could not allow himself time

off either for years of theological study or for the changes of residence required if the development of remote brotherhoods is to be ensured. Only the community of the Church as a whole and her organisation makes this possible. But if this is so, the result no longer depends upon us; it will depend upon the Church's own mission operating through the Brotherhoods. We know that the duty of working for the expansion of the Church is incumbent upon every member of the mystical body; every member has his part to play. When we ask for material aid to help us to carry out our special missionary calling, we are not really asking for alms, but confronting such Christians as can bear it with a duty to be performed according to their ability.

Whatever the means we use we must maintain a spirit of poverty and simplicity. But inasmuch as we are servants of the Church we may not arbitrarily limit the extent of the progress of our Brotherhoods. Our calling to the hidden life does not necessarily mean that the life of the Petits Frères must remain utterly secret; the inference is quite different. The incredible popularity of the Franciscan movement when it began and the social upheaval it involved, was no obstacle to the poverty, humility, and lowly form of life of the first companions and disciples of the poor little man of Assisi. Let us remain unassuming and unsophisticated so as to be always ready to carry out any command our Lord may lay upon us.

The expansion of Christ's love throughout the world and the poverty of the workman of Nazareth are thus like the two poles of our vocation. It is in order that you may be prepared to carry out the first aspect of your mission more worthily that you must be willing to spend several years as a student. Nothing is more natural than that you should have strong and painful feelings at being unable to work with the poor. This may be all to the good, provided you do not think it implies a lowering of your ideal, and provided you give yourselves wholeheartedly to your studies. Do not toy with

the idea of some kind of compromise between living as a
student and living as a worker, for that would prevent you
from taking full advantage of your studies. After all, being
a student is a form of poverty: it means that one is either a
pensioner of the state or else maintained by private or organised
goodwill. Your position will be no different! You will have
to be willing to be maintained by your brethren or by other
Christians . . .

Strasbourg, 13 March

1952

Today is Easter day, the great, the unique Christian festival! The apostles' testimony was, in its entirety, based upon this fact: Jesus is risen. Their faith is utterly dependent upon this certainty, and without it, we should be, as St. Paul said, the most wretched of mankind.

In the world, we must be *witnesses of the resurrection of Jesus.* To bear witness to love, to the reality of a life according to the gospel, is a great thing, but it is not enough if we are not also witnesses to the faith, witnesses to the fact of Christ's resurrection. I am thinking of the future, and I see you spread throughout a materialistic world in which there will no longer be room in public life and in the organisation of factory work for any object or activity whose purpose is to bear witness to a religious fact. Should the time come when Christians live outwardly as though they did not believe, as though Christ had not risen, if they agreed to allow the machinery of soul-destroying labour to swamp their most important religious festivals, then mankind would have no visible witness to belief in the risen Lord. This would be extremely serious for us, for the Brotherhoods. For the nature of any witness implies that it can be seen. The festival of our Lord's resurrection should make us realise what Christianity demands from us, and, with especial force, the impact of our mission as witnesses of our Lord.

Yesterday evening a trifling incident made me understand

more acutely than ever before the danger that threatens us. Some of you allowed yourselves to become involved in manual work that was certainly urgent but not indispensable, and were consequently absent from the general meeting of all the brethren on Holy Saturday evening, and even worked for a while on Easter Day.

You know how strongly I feel that our vocation demands that on ordinary days we should be ready for anything, however unexpected. But that no greater effort should be made at Christmas or Easter to secure a stoppage of material work in order that the anniversaries of our Lord's birth and resurrection might retain their full significance, seems to me to display a lack of sincerity and courage in our witness to the faith. If we are people who in the midst of the world believe absolutely in Christ's birth and resurrection, then these two anniversaries must matter so much that we could not fail to give them a realistic expression, especially in a civilisation in which the meaning of these beliefs no longer counts.

How can men really believe that we believe, if on such days as these we make no outward sign of our faith? A testimony is due to our Lord which we dare not refuse. Do not argue from the fact that other men are content to go to work on these days. Keep free of human respect. Your desire to share the lot of the working masses must stop short at the levelling down of your life to the stage when you have to give up those obligations which belief imposes. On this Easter Day I pray that one grace of this mystery may be the bestowal of a faith in all the Brotherhoods that will give them the requisite courage and pride to affirm it freely wherever necessary. It is an attitude that may be at odds with the contemporary environment, but it is fundamentally related to the demands made upon us as disciples of our Lord: 'Are not you also one of this man's disciples?' (John 18:17).

El-Abiodh-Sidi-Cheikh, 13 April

When I was looking through some of the documents relating to the Rule of St. Pachomius and the organisation of his earliest monasteries in the Egyptian desert, I came across a series of counsels given by Pachomius to his 'heads of houses'. The monasteries were like villages; the monks were usually grouped according to their crafts (there were weavers, blacksmiths, boatmen, wheelwrights, smallholders, etc.). Each group formed a kind of neighbourhood with a superior who was called 'the head of the house'. I was impressed by the extremely human and realistic nature of the saint's advice: he advocated a strong will, honesty, temperate behaviour, uprightness, respect for the poor and for children, sincerity, unremitting work.

This is a sound and Christian idea of monastic perfection and it provokes the question as to whether some contemporary ideas do not need revision. A perfect monk is a perfect Christian and a perfect Christian is a perfect man. The divine life cannot abolish natural human perfection; it sanctifies it. How much imbalance, what distortion of the idea of perfection has resulted from forgetting this! Without any exception, we are all compelled to acquire these simple and essential virtues which contribute to the make-up of the perfect man.

As for us, given our vocation this an indispensable foundation. Any man who rejects or neglects human perfection can never be a perfect disciple of Christ. I have previously felt bound to mention this to you when I thought that you were being negligent about certain human characteristics. Giving these up is far more often an indication of a lack of courage, than of forgetfulness of this world for the sake of the world to come. The gospel sounds no such note; it is far too human. We should never forget that it completes and *fulfils* the old Law, but destroys nothing in it. Very often we try to put up the building without first digging its foundations. The Law given on Sinaï was, as our Lord pointed out, an expression of love. To build so-called religious perfection by means of a series of regulations, exercises, and even of lengthy periods of prayer, while forgetting to lay the solid and balanced foundation made up of every element that goes to the formation of a man according to God's heart, is to produce a real caricature of what the gospel means by perfection. Jesus told the rich young man to leave all and follow him, only after he had secured his admission that he was observing the whole Law . . . No 'supernatural' virtue can be a substitute for [the] human virtues (which in a Christian *are* supernatural because they are achieved through love): they are a language which true love cannot do without.

Cairo, 17 November

The [holy places in Palestine] sharply confront us with the earthly reality of the mystery of our Lord's life and death, and through them we come to realise the feebleness of our faith. We find it easy enough to say: 'Lord, Lord,' and yet still do not believe. If our Lord does not seem to us to belong to the real world, is it surprising that his words no longer affect our lives? If they are to take us out of the rut of custom and deliver us from its bondage, those words must come alive. Otherwise, they are far from being the sword that penetrates to the very muscles of our daily behaviour.

Our Lord is not in fact a real individual for us, a living person. Dare we say that we belong to him, that we give him our lives? Well, here we are faced with the places where he lived, died his agonising death, and came out of the grave alive. That since these events took place, days, or years, or centuries have passed, is immaterial. These places make one feel infinitely empty and squalid, appallingly egotistic and hidebound in routine and comformity. I am reminded of Peter who in this very place declared that he did not know Jesus, and of the other apostles who the moment he was arrested and brought to judgement, made themselves scarce. I should have been among them, and God knows whether . . .!

Jerusalem has not altered since my last visit. What was dilapidated remains so. The Holy Sepulchre is perhaps the only Christian sanctuary in the world propped up by a mass of wood and iron scaffolding, and looking as though the intention of maintaining it had been given up. It is always almost empty, and few people come to this place where their Friend, their greatest Friend and the Lord their God, once died, in order to pray there and meditate a little on the wonder of these events and kiss the rock of the tomb out of which their life came forth!

I found this desolation all the more striking after I had travelled round the world. Everywhere else there is life; but not here. The great American cities are alive. Men cross the world and travel more than ever; everywhere buildings are going up; factories, churches, and monasteries are being built all over the world; and the Church of the Resurrection is falling into ruins! Crowds throng in a multitude of pilgrimages, but the land of Jesus no longer attracts anybody! What friend of Christ and of our Lady can fail to be saddened at such neglect?

There are, of course, places in the world filled with human suffering; there are devastated cities, countries where men are slaughtering each other. But the land of Christ gives an impression of stagnation, abandonment, and gradual decay, as though the only material remains on earth of the visit of the Word incarnate no longer interested anybody, neither states or Christian people, or even the clergy. In the last twenty years, how many bishops have paid a visit to Christ's grave?

Jerusalem remains divided into two. Weeds are there and grass grows in the rubble of the houses, situated between the two lines, and that no one can rebuild.

Who is concerned for the future of this land covered with tents that each year become a little more dilapidated, under which dwell the Arabs who have fled from Palestine? Our Lord's homeland is surrounded by a belt of misery which every day the world more easily takes as normal and for which there seems no hope. The efforts of the United Nations have not even succeeded in securing land, work, and a human existence for these forlorn families, some of whom daily climb up Mount Sion and, in tears, look down upon their houses and fields which for three years have been inaccessible to them.

How has it come about that we have become so insensitive to the interests of our Lord's homeland and to the earthly reminders of his life? The crowds of pilgrims go elsewhere, to Lourdes, Fatima, Rome, and many of them, led by their bishops, do not hesitate to go to remote eucharistic congresses, even as far as the antipodes. So it is not only a question of distance. Too few Christians really wish to make this pilgrimage. Do those who are in fact unable to make it, regret the fact? How many would do as much to go once in their lives to pray at Calvary and on the Mount of Olives, as many Mohammedans do in order to go to Mecca?

When this mentality is compared with that of medieval Christianity which, in spite of its defects, was ready to do all in its power to deliver the Holy Sepulchre, it suggests that there is something lacking in the belief of contemporary Christians.

I may be told, however, that this is not all that important, and that the magnificent development of Catholic Action, the Christian resurgence to be seen in a great number of countries, and the courage of so many Christians in confessing their faith or in facing persecution, is of greater significance than a pilgrimage to the Holy Land and indicates that God's people are really alive . . .

I do not mean to assert that there is less life in the Church today, or less generosity and love. It is never just to make comparisons or allow oneself to form a judgement about things which only God can know.

Nevertheless, we have the right to look for the source of this easy forgetfulness of the only earthly and visible reminder of Christ, in a deviation in our spiritual outlook. Our religion is no longer focused to the same extent upon the actual person of Christ. The systems of spirituality have perhaps become too abstract or complex, and the preaching of religion excessively moralistic. The most unalloyed morality or the most generous activity of love, if allowed to lose their close relationship with the person of Christ the Saviour, immediately begin to undergo changes which are not without their remote repercussions on the general life of mankind. In so far as our spiritual development really has our Lord as its goal, in that same degree unity among Christians grows deeper and even the divisions that affect the Church are lessened. A Protestant pastor of some of our friends wrote recently to one of the brothers: 'It is so true that the nearer we approach to our Lord, the nearer we approach to each other.'

All of us have been gathered together through the challenge of the life of . . . Brother Charles of Jesus and have been led by him to a simple and direct love of our saviour, and we must rediscover that way of life that is entirely focused upon him. This will entail no loss in the quality of the love we give to man. In Father de Foucauld's life, the love of Palestine, the desire to go and stay there, were factors of great importance. Jerusalem, Bethlehem, Nazareth, all contributed to that simplicity, as translucent and enduring as crystal, which characterised his relationships with Christ, our Lady, and the saints contemporary with [them].

I am not saying that all of you will be able one day to make the great pilgrimage. But you must love our Lord in such a way that you will wholeheartedly want to do so. Why should

you not? Why not have the courage to undertake it in poverty?
I am certain that if we really wanted it, many would find themselves able to go there, once in a lifetime. It would provide an
example. It would be the means of reawakening a more vivid
consciousness of the reality of the Man-God and of ending
the scandalous fact that perhaps no sanctuary in the world is
so forsaken as that of the death and resurrection of their 'well-
beloved brother and Lord, Jesus'.

Jerusalem, 28 November

Confronted by the vast extent of the wretched conditions
of life endured by the people [of India] and the human problem
that this presents, I have again considered what should be the
standpoint of the Brotherhoods in an environment like this
and what Father de Foucauld, who realised so thoroughly
that a minimum standard of human existence is indispensable
for Christian living, would have expected from us . . .

A Brotherhood can be put into a false position, if the attitude of the brethren is purely negative. With all the impetus of
his generous soul, Father de Foucauld yearned for his Petits
Frères to become an element of enlightenment and progress,
even of human progress, in environments such as this which
will be crushed by human development, if they cannot adapt
themselves to technical progress.

I can only repeat what our Constitutions lay down: by
means of their work the brethren must become incorporated
with those around them and raise their standards. They remain the brothers of these men if the work they undertake is
always accessible to them. When the gospel is carried out in a
life of love, it cannot be an example of human passivity and
want of effort; that would make it hateful. It must be a sound
and healthy leaven for human values that may not be sump-
tuous, but are nevertheless true.

As we have previously remarked, this amounts to saying
that we must be careful not to describe our calling as contem-

platives in the world in terms of the negative values of flight. For instance, it is sometimes said that because the Petits Frères must resemble the poor around them, they must not teach, preach, do good works, try to raise the local standard of living, or be over-zealous in offering their services, for such a demonstration of superior efficiency in the loving service of others would be a cause of separation from them. If to this fundamentally negative attitude we add mediocrity of soul, then it is a catastrophe indeed! I am always having to protest against the definition given by well-meaning people who are anxious to explain our way of life to those who are to receive us: 'The Petits Frères are not engaged in this activity or that; they must not be involved in anything, but simply give an example.' It is a wooden and detestable definition . . .

Our vocation needs to be defined *positively*, by means of those worthwhile realities which our lives must express: namely, the wish to be united with our Lord, the wish to be like him in poverty and in work, to remain the brother and friend of the poor and not to rise above them and to be ready for every demand made by love as it loyally follows our Lord in his prayer and humility, so that we may help our brethren to emerge from their passive hopelessness and misery . . .

Delhi, 19 December

1953

The gravity of [the crisis of the Worker-Priests in France] is obvious, but I believe that although the Church has drawn our attention to certain errors or deviations, she has not dispensed us from facing the immense problem that has arisen not only in France but throughout the world, from the fact that countless human beings are now in a position of being crushed by a technical civilisation no longer in control of itself, nor able, on account of its structure and of the speed it has acquired, to envisage economic problems primarily in their human aspect. Everywhere it is business, productivity, and the development of the means of production, that is crushing man. What I recently experienced in Kenya and what I see here in the Transvaal appals me. I would not have believed that the results of colonial exploitation could be so cruel and inhuman. Men seem to be like playthings caught in the determinism of a soulless civilisation. Christians have no right to make little of facts like these.

Johannesburg, 22 September

Today is the feast of the patronage of St. Thomas, in the Dominican calendar. During the mass celebrated in this Church constructed of earth, and among these poor and very simple cultivators [in the heart of Brazil, at the last stage of the populated area], I could not help reflecting on the nature of human wisdom and wondering where it is to be found.

196

My thoughts turn to the heaped-up human masses in the cities, the host of workers, the inevitable slavery involved in supplying man-made human needs, in the race for an ever-rising standard of living. I am thinking especially of the mentality which such an existence gradually produces, the materialisation that results from it, the absence of peace, the destruction of the healthiest or most human spiritual responses which, however, are still to be found in 'primitive' men.

It is just here that the Marxist theory of scientific civilisation is more erroneous and anti-human than in any other aspect. I see why it is essentially anti-religious. The terrible thing is that in the end this is not even realised. The oppression of poor and simple people by those who control commerce, technical industry, or capital, is itself hateful enough. It can either be the expression of overpowering egoism or be done unconsciously, and both forms are evident here . . . But what seems to me frightening in Marxism (as in racial or other kinds of totalitarianism) is its attempt to affect man in his very nature. Its aim is to create a new type of man, to remake man, give his mind a new pattern, annihilate some of his responses. To attempt to alter this living and spiritual organism, made in God's image, is a terrible thing when the approach to this mystery is made by means of the instruments provided by a materialist technique.

Whatever might be valid in such an undertaking to renew mankind is rendered null and void, simply because the work of altering the most sensitive and sacred elements in human beings is being entrusted to clumsy hands, helped by materialistic techniques. Under the pretext of creating a human civilisation and of escaping from the slavery of industrial capitalism, the process has begun of destroying or nullifying man himself. After this treatment men are left with the loss of their God-given moral consciousness, the loss of their belief, and often of their need for a living and personal God.

I assure you that once I had left the stranglehold of this kind of 'thought' far behind me, once I had become familiar with the most different types of people throughout the world, I saw this danger with unmistakable clarity.

The grip maintained by unlicensed capitalism over peoples that are socially developed is less brutal in some countries, more violent and primitive in others. But whatever the facts of this oppression, it can never, in any circumstances, be lawful to try and deliver us from it by interfering with human nature, under the pretext of enabling it to adapt itself to a new kind of social life, entirely man-made, according to a rigid and totalitarian pattern that excludes all freedom.

This mystery of man which had already been interfered with externally by technical civilisation, and which Marxism now attacks in its spiritual centre, was nothing like so obvious to me before I had come in contact with those we call 'primitive' men ... I believe that we have reached one of the most perilous moments in the history of mankind. For the first time, men have acquired the power of interfering with the mystery of human nature itself, using all the technical resources put into their hands by the social, economic, medical, and psychological sciences. It is no longer simply a question of social dictatorship, a planned economy, transfers of population, and tests for professional pursuits; we are going much farther now, and an attempt is being made to 'rethink' man himself, to give him an entirely new adaptation, in the way that the most complex machine tools are brought to their perfection.

Rio Araguaya, 13 November

1956

As I wander alone on my travels I am learning many things, but I daily become more aware of the mystery of the world, of mankind divided against itself. Is our Lord present amidst it all? One looks for him in this multitude of thousands of millions of men. Sin at any rate is present. There is the sin of the rich, and the mystery of the poor who see no way out. These pagan multitudes of India, this teeming mass of physical and moral misery, and this ignorance of the true mystery of the gracious God again and again appals me. And yet even in this poverty something other than this wretched existence is being looked for and there is a felt need for purification. The water of the Ganges is no more than dull and muddy water, but for the crowds it is the mysterious sign of that which they are seeking.

I have a growing horror of the sin of materialism of our civilisation and immense pity for all those peoples of the West who are so sure of themselves that they appear to be looking for nothing beyond. Their sin may on that account be all the greater, but they do not see it. They themselves do not see it. They have wanted too much from this world and have received it; they are too rich.

Benares, 8 April

1957

I greatly value the chapel of the Brotherhood in Marseilles, because it is wholly Byzantine and because the icons in it create a kind of presence of the invisible world. I find that these icons are a great help in bringing me into the company of those who are invisibly taking part in the eucharistic sacrifice and in uniting me with their offering. The keener we are to make a humble use of the means of uniting ourselves with those who dwell in the supernatural world, the better we shall appreciate the importance attached by the Church to those earthly representations of the invisible, which is what our chapels must be. We are *present* in this world, but we are also *on the look-out* for another world which is coming, and without the thought of which we cannot believe in, hope for, and love our Lord. *Lord Jesus, come!* Those who had seen the Lord were ready to wait for him. That day will come quickly.

Marseilles, 20 October

It is startling to realise the degree in which painting is an expression of the mystery of the incarnation. We cannot do without the faces of our Lord and our Lady, and pictorial and sculptural representations of the mysteries of their lives. It was long before I understood the real explanation of the resistance, even at the cost of their lives, made by Christians against the heresy of the iconoclasts, the image-breakers. It now seems to me obvious that the condemnation of representations of our Lord, our Lady, and the saints was like a denial of one of the consequences of the incarnation of the Word, a consequence God intended. Why should the contemporaries of Jesus and Mary have been the only ones to cherish the faces which made the reality of our relationship with God manifest to us? Contempt for images or their systematic rejection is an indication of our failure to understand how completely we need the presence of our Lord's face in our daily life, like a constant reminder that now and for ever God has a human face to see us and listen to us, and a human heart to love us with.

Abstract religious art that deliberately rejects any suggestion of the human face of him whose precise purpose in assuming it was to express his love for us, is no longer Christian art, inasmuch as it entails a refusal to express our Lord's presence among us, in its human truth. Since the special characteristic of our religion is a Christ who is the saviour, true God, and true man, Christian art is constantly being asked, on pain of not being authentic, to express simultaneously the infinite and formless grandeur of the majesty of the invisible God and the wonderfully human face of Jesus. It is an undertaking whose difficulty explains the constant search for fresh means and the indefinitely renewed experimentation of an art that will never be able to express the mystery of the Man-God completely. Before the incarnation the prohibition of graven images was a means of instilling the idea of the real nature of the transcendent God in believers' minds. Some mosques have an impressive grandeur of art and are admirably pure in form and unadorned. They are peaks of art and of religious expression, but they may be said to shut out the incarnation of the Word. They cannot be Christian.

Florence, 24 December

1958

Although it may seem a somewhat terrestrial interest, a word must be said about nutrition in the Brotherhoods. It is a question less important for working Brotherhoods in temperate climates than for those in the tropics or those containing a great number of brethren. It may even be morally wrong to fail to take into account the elementary natural laws on human nutrition, when grave and sometimes final consequences for man's spiritual equilibrium may follow from their neglect.

Loyalty to our vocation entails far more complex problems in this sphere than it does in other forms of the religious life. Today the essential laws of nutrition are known, therefore it may well be a duty not merely to learn what they are, but also to try to observe them, insofar as no more compelling obligation prevents us. In fact, if we are to remain truly poor, then, at least to some extent, we must observe the elementary requirements of a balanced diet which alone will give us staying power and the ability to work. Incidentally it is untrue that a balanced and healthy regime must be an expensive one, opposed to poverty. In any case in our time it is now no longer permissible to despise the laws of nutrition and to make it a point of honour or a principle of poverty to eat no matter what. The young might indeed be able to exist for two or three years, relying in this way on their reserves, and then find themselves radically unfit.

The deliberate neglect of these laws . . . is quite a different matter from the acceptance of serious danger to health as the result of living in a difficult climate out of love for those who dwell in it. In spite of every effort it may well prove impossible to provide all that is essential for the body's needs. At the same time the utmost must be done to avoid this risk. It is almost always possible to improve a diet by making use of the country's resources. Indeed, the attempt to do this may also prove beneficial to native peoples accustomed to a defective diet and unable to remedy it themselves, through ignorance of what is required for bodily health. An effort of this kind, likely to be accepted by the natives, must not be considered alien to the vocation of the Brotherhoods. Conformity to the Creator's laws for human spiritual and bodily equilibrium is, in fact, a form of obedience to him, and an habitual infringement of these laws, without adequate reason, cannot fail to involve our moral responsibility. The essential thing is to do everything possible to approximate to a balanced diet: this is the best way to expel all excessive worry about food.

Toulouse, 16 April

I am staying his evening and tonight in the bishop's palace in Münster, and I have been able to have a long conversation with the bishop. It was a great comfort to discover his understanding of the Brotherhood's vocation, and the breadth of his vision of the Church's apostolate.

We talked a great deal about *the position of the working class and about the problem of its evangelisation*. The situation which inspired the movement of the Worker-Priests does not yet exist in other European countries. In a nation all of whose people, Catholics or Protestants, are baptised, the nucleus of the religious sense remains alive . . . It is hard to realise how important is the presence in France of so many unbelievers, whether Marxist or not, who have not been baptised and are practical if not theoretical atheists.

It became increasingly clear to me that the Church has what may be called two fronts for her apostolate, and that this fact necessitates two different kinds of evangelisation. It means that one cannot dedicate oneself to either of these two missions without bothering which of them it is. One of them is concerned with sustaining or renewing the Christianity of people who are believers or at least baptised; the other is to proclaim the gospel to those who, apparently, no longer experience any need for religion, expect nothing from it and whose rationally organised universe excludes the very idea of God.

Some regions may belong as a whole to one or other of these fronts, and the problem of the apostolate then presents itself in the same terms to all the clergy or to those who have received an apostolic mission from the Church. But as a rule the two fronts are intricately combined within the area of a single people. There may be zones in which all the people are practically atheists, but what may be called Christian zones in which godless atheism is not already present, do not exist. So far it may not be on the surface, but beneath conduct that is still apparently Christian, pagan points of view or lines of behaviour are erupting. We are witnessing the birth pangs of a new world, the leaven of practical atheism is everywhere in ferment and the tide sweeps in.

Münster, 5 June

1959

Easter means the living, divine, humanly glorious presence of our Lord, together with the certainty that one day we shall be *like him*, with our lowly body glorified like his. A firm belief in this brings great joy and a well-grounded hope. It will very soon be experienced by each one of us. I pray that on this day of his resurrection, our Lord may implant this certitude like a grace in the depth of your hearts. This expectation, this immediate expectation, must have its influence over our entire life: there will be another world, another life, another land. This is the certitude that Easter provides.

I greatly value that presence of the supernatural world, of the holiness of Jesus, of the apostles and the saints, into which every aspect of a Russian church and the Byzantine liturgy introduces us. This is not the crystallisation of a nostalgic dream provoked by the dreariness of life in this sad world; it is not an escape; it is an already existing reality into which we shall enter at no distant date. I am reminded of all the hidden suffering of those who, in Russia, are trying to maintain this hope, this assurance of the other world, the world of the risen Christ, against the slow dissolution imposed by a now triumphant materialism that is realistic and tangible in its achievements in this world, and sure of being the one reality that can cope with the nostalgic dreams of a future paradise, dreams that foster a passivity injurious to the progress of mankind.

The Lord is risen, nothing is more sure, he awaits us, he is there; and this is the hope, the joy, and *the essential reason* for our religious dedication . . .

San Francisco, 28 March

I am beginning to realise the extent to which we are under an obligation to live *now*, *in the present moment*. In the life of every man two spheres exist: that of *the dream* and that of *reality*. These are very often so combined that we cannot clearly distinguish between them! The dream is that which we imagine: false ideas about ourselves, delusions, the refusal to accept others as they really are, evil desires sustained by imaginary satisfactions, the urge to believe that we are other than we are. All these imaginative ruminations, these fantasies, embed us in ourselves. It is impossible to live alone with one-self without dreaming, at least unless one is with God.

As for reality, we find it hard to accept its truth, since it compels us to accept the cross and to open ourselves to others. Those *others*, our brethren, form that part of reality which penetrates our inmost being. When we open ourselves to others, and genuinely enter into communication with them, we escape from dreaming and begin to ring true. Dreaming of love is not real love. 'It is not those who say: "Lord, Lord," who will enter the Kingdom of Heaven, but those who do . . .'

The reality of existence on this earth is made up for each of us of several worlds. First, we have ourselves, with our defects and limitations, with the pull of the flesh, but also with the goodness of our will. This is our own, our personal world. Secondly, there is the external world, stable and tangible, with its painful or happy events—what is called *life*. It is a world that contains other people, other men in their objective reality. Why should we resist the necessity of honestly accepting this world as it is, and especially other men, our brothers, as they are, in flesh and blood, and not as they ought to be, or as we imagine they ought to be, but with both their defects and their qualities, and be ready to love them as such? Jesus knew the whole truth about every man; he had no need to be told about it; he had no illusions—and yet he loved them . . .

And lastly, and above all, there is the great reality which is God. This is the world of the risen, living Lord, and of all the invisible realities which bind us to him. This invisible world is supernatural; but it is not a dream; it is reality in its absolutely concrete form.

To live *now, this instant,* is to welcome these three realities: ourselves, the external world, the universe of other men, and that over which our Lord reigns . . . [It means] that we refuse to escape into dreams either of the past, the future, or the unreal . . . A man gains spiritual health when he is in possession of the present moment and no longer indulges in dreams of escaping from it, but steps out into the daylight of Him who made all things and all life's passing moments and said that *they were good.* The cross of Calvary which was a harsh but real moment transformed everything that harms us in this world into a source of perennial good. Do not be afraid to become a living being, to grasp the present moment with both hands, and to make it utterly your own.

We often dream that we are better than we are. Who has not dreamt that he is a saint, a great man, or a martyr? Sometimes this does us good; in order to make the dream real we make an effort to overcome the difficulties of the present moment and the temptations lurking in it. But if a dream does have such efficacy, this is because it almost deserves the name of *hope.*

Our Lord presents the perfect image of what we must become: a son of God and his own brother. This is no longer a dream; it means that we have made a preliminary contact with a reality that will show us the way to go and give us the strength to travel. A dream which is a mere mirage prevents us living *now,* but hope enables us to participate in God's dream for us and accept what is in front of us with patience and energy. The idea of God's presence within us is no dream; to abandon oneself, to put oneself completely at God's service, is to acquire the ability to pass from day-dreaming into truth . . .

Moment by moment we must allow ourselves to be guided by *the present*, by those outside us, or by God, his providence or his voice in the gospel. If we concentrate our meagre resources on this present moment, it becomes luminous, almost easy, and always possible. Also this is essentially more worthwhile than dreaming because the undoubted reality of other people and of external events introduces us to the cross and to the reality of God. In my own life I have only two alternatives: either I am being disturbed, consumed by other people, constantly on the move from one place, one house to another, always packing or unpacking my suitcase, or, should I refuse to accept this, then I would become alone, absolutely alone. In any case, if I turn away from reality, I either start living in the future and cease to be able to give myself completely, or else I shut myself up in my dreams with God excluded. But if I enter fully into the reality of the present moment, I give myself joyfully to others because I allow them to come into my life, just as they are. By opening out a pathway into me, they deliver me from myself and give me to God. When, however, I am by myself, I must allow the reality of God to enter. Never must we be *alone*. When someone apologised for letting him wait a few moments alone, Brother Charles could not help exclaiming spontaneously: 'But I am never alone!' He was living in the embrace of reality. When we *are* really alone, without our intimate and abiding Friend, it is an indication that something has gone wrong; we are turning away from reality. We must hasten to regain contact with a presence: either that of men or God. Inward solitude leaves us a prey to every evil desire that stirs within us and we settle down in our egotistic dream world. Try to infuse yourself body and soul into the passing minute, so that it may be energised with life. Give an attentive heart to your life as, minute by minute, God gives it to you. You will never again recover this moment that has been given you to live . . .

Le Carbet, 25 April

I am thinking, today, of a group of young people I met at Montevideo, mostly students, some of them married, some already started on their professional life. I was moved by their keenness and generosity, their desire to submit their life in its entirety to the guidance of faith, even to the extent of pooling their resources. One of the questions they asked keeps on recurring to me: they longed for a life that could be lived together in perfect unity and wanted me to tell them what they must do in order that every aspect of their lives might be co-ordinated in unity: their prayer, their professional and political activities, their family life. How could all these extremely different activities be unified?

Do we not all crave for a life all of whose elements cohere in unity? But I am very much afraid that the ideas of unity which these young people have formed will make its achievement impossible. I tried to explain this to them because I was afraid that they might experience one disillusionment after another and end up in despair. For if by unity we mean the psychological and emotional unity of our lives, this is something we cannot integrally attain.

Our Lord even inserted *contradiction* and not unity into our lives, the moment he became part of them. What, in fact, does this word *unity* mean in the context of the slender resources of human consciousness? Unity demands that peace and order shall be in complete control of ourselves and of human society. But two men exist in us: the flesh fights against the spirit. Sensual and emotional love blind the spirit seeking the love of God. Not unity but conflict is the reality. So long as we are subject to the conditions of this world, *the unity* of our life can mean no more than the resolve that God shall reign over our whole being: 'Where your treasure is, there your heart will be . . . you cannot serve two masters at once.' This is the only principle of unity accessible to us.

On earth we may not indulge in the dream of a harmonious and unified life because the fellowship of those among whom we live, even if we live in a religious community, is not yet established in that order and peace which results from unalterable devotion to a single love.

The vocation of the Petits Frères, more than any other, puts us at the heart of the contradiction in the world, at its storm centre, because we are deposited on the spot where an attempt is being made to implant the contemplation of the invisible and crucified God in the daily life of mankind. Around us we shall find no unified existence, and we shall succeed in introducing the principle of it in ourselves only if we cease to depend upon the world and our physical senses and ascend above the subjective psychological plane. Those who try to achieve unity on that plane are endangering the supernatural soaring of their life's profoundest elements.

There are, in fact, only two ways of achieving a psychological unity between a life of prayer and our human contacts. We can either carry over our anxieties and the tender memories of our brethren into our prayer; in which case that prayer runs the risk of becoming not a contemplation of God alone but a summary of everything that binds us to mankind. Or, in our human intercourse, we can try to maintain the same aloofness from the concerns of the senses as in prayer; and in that case our presence among men runs the risk of ceasing to be human and true.

It may well be that only eremitical monks, such as the Carthusians, can hope to secure at least a kind of unity in their external lives while still on earth. As for their inner lives, they remain, until the resurrection, subject to the same conditions as those of all the children of Adam. I have often observed how compulsively the young are drawn to try to obtain psychological unity in their religious life and find it hard to steer clear of the Scylla and Charybdis just noted. We shall be making progress towards the unity that will come when our body is glorified, in the degree in which we strive to establish the empire of a single love within us. This will not be done without a struggle, for in this life we shall never have more than the first shoots of the life of glory.

Belo Horizonte (Brazil), 7 July

I have just paid a visit to a family who are friends of mine. The mother, who is still young, with four children, has been attacked by cancer and she has only a few months to live. She knows quite well the approximate date for her departure and awaits it with serene peace and in admirably good spirits. She is still leading a very active life and anyone not informed would not suspect anything. I was greatly moved at finding her so close to that sublime paradise about which we all wonder how it will fare with us.

We have difficulty in imagining it, and especially in convincing ourselves that it is a reality close at hand, a matter of months or even days. What really ultimate difference exists between this mother's case and our own? We may even cross life's threshold before her; but she *knows*, she *awaits*, accompanied by the certainty of the time of her journey. Everything she now does may be said to have had a new light thrown upon it by her approaching death. She no longer looks in the same way upon the world, her home, the well known things around her, her daily tasks, her husband—very sad, but courageous—her children, who are full of fun and unaware of their coming loss. How this makes us realise that death and the life after it is something that increases the greatness of man! It reveals the whole mystery of our life. *She* knows when her death will be and awaits it, and because of this we approach her with respect and emotion. And yet, each of us should also *know* and *wait*. The thought of death ought to be the source of our strength and of our immense significance. For man alone, of all living beings, *knows* that he must die. Does the date matter? It is just as near, and this nearness is momentous.

Some religious orders have held that the 'preparation for death' forms an essential element in every monthly retreat. Today we tend to consider such an exercise as artificial and no longer worthwhile. If it *is* merely an exercise, this is no doubt true. But the thought of death, of our own death, is a great matter. Our Lord knew beforehand when he would die, he knew every detail of his death, and this thought was an integral part of his human consciousness. We do not dwell upon death sufficiently; we are not sufficiently aware that our outlook upon the world and our fellow men would alter if we knew that our death was near at hand.

We ought to think not only of death in general but also of our own death, for that gives everything its true perspective and makes us stronger and more worthwhile. If we are expecting another form of life we shall live this life on earth more intensely, for that expectation wholly determines the way we live now. The departure through death of those we love and with whom we have lived intimately, is a reminder that that other Life is at hand. We should cherish this reminder and periodically renew it.

Brazil, 9 July

I had just been reading in a local paper the final technical details of the interplanetary station Lunik III, when glancing cursorily through an article on the Church in [modern] Israel I came across the following lines: 'Holy Scripture puts before us a wonderful vision of a future of unity and peace' in which 'there will be only one flock and one shepherd'. It will be a day of such joy for mankind that St. Paul compares it to a new life springing out of death.

I ask myself what we are likely to feel about such a prospect today. Is it a 'poetical' fancy that has little to do with the very concrete reality amidst which we live? This picture of mankind's destiny seems so remote and hardly credible. What future would there be for the Church on earth in these times to come. Will she really one day extend her kingdom over most men?

Another question is that of the general resurrection. When will it really happen? Is it not true that when we think this out, our imagination fails ... What will you and I be like when it does occur? How in actual fact will mankind exist after this renewal, encumbered as it must be by the countless millions who have spent their brief existence on this earth? ... How will Christ come? How will he be bodily present to all men and to each individual man? What will he do as a man, and what will these multitudes do as human beings? In what way shall we see our Lord and his mother? And what kind of relationship with our Lord will these millions of people, all of them alive at once, be able to establish?

We dare not put all these questions too insistently to our wavering faith; and yet, while men are devoting their lives to the preparation of an immediate and attractive future for mankind, what goal are *we* able to propose for our lives? For *if* we do not succeed in establishing an affective relationship of cause and effect between this Christian vision of mankind's resurrection and the reasons for our way of living and acting *now*, and for as long as we are on earth, how shall we be able to accept the imperatives of the gospel, and where shall we find the strength to live as our saviour asks us to?

To give up this world's pleasures, some of its joys and accept suffering as a source of life, is all very well, but when are we going to experience this true life? How can we believe in the reign of love among men when everywhere we behold divisions, hatred, self-satisfied injustice, the tragic consequences of egotism? How can we make up our minds to disregard some of the facts around us and *to wait for* a result of our activity, a result in the distant future, outside and above our present field of knowledge and perception? We are living in a way exactly the reverse of that of other men!

How much nearer the whole of this world to come must have seemed at a time when the common human outlook was open to the realities of religion, life flowed along with a slow and gentle rhythm, and no vast terrestrial or scientific prospect had so swelled the dimensions of *this* life, from birth to death, that there is no longer any room for interest in *another*. Another life! How uncertain, remote, and absurd that seems!

How can we believe that it serves any useful purpose to teach men to love one another, even though they fail to achieve such love on earth, if we are not certain that this beginning is but germinal and that though the seed must be sown now, its fruit will be ready for harvesting only at a much later date? The whole crop will be cut later on. A Christian existence, or a life devoted to the invisible, is only a preliminary sketch, a beginning of the true life which is coming but is not yet here.

The difficulties encountered in the religious and especially the contemplative life, are for the most part due to this lack of certainty about the life to come. Our motives for acting are neither clear nor sufficiently real! If these motives, and also the joy we seek, are exclusively contained within the limits of our earthly life, then we absolutely cannot succeed [in the religious life]. We may manage to carry on by means of constant restraint imposed without any counterpart in our most natural and spontaneous human desires. There will then be no real fulfilment for us. Or, on the other hand, we may give up altogether, abandoning all constraint by the dictates of faith. And when I speak of motives for living contained within the limits of our earthly existence I definitely do not mean to exclude those motives—even the most lofty ones—often proposed to Christians as a stimulus to their life or their apostolic activity, such as, for example, the missionary achievements of the Church on earth, the establishment of justice and charity among men. It is possible to offer and even sacrifice one's life for such goals, and some do achieve this end successfully.

But fundamentally there are deep desires within us which remain unsatisfied. The Church's most successful achievements on earth are themselves only preliminary sketches, just as the partial achievements of justice and charity are the preliminary sketch of the charity of another earthly city. Apart from some very pure and very rare moments when we are allowed to contemplate God's glory in Christ, there is a danger that even in our most Christian activities, we may find ourselves outside the essential hope. And yet we are certainly bound to come back to this hope, when we are confronted by our sinfulness, by the supreme issues of loss and gain in our life, by the cross of our powerlessness, at last realised as final —and our own death.

When our Lord was in his death agony on the gallows, he saw the coming of this Kingdom, as if it was already present, and that is why he had the strength to consummate the whole of his present life as a man and make it a perfect offering. He was in haste to rise again, he was certain that he would, for his own sake and ours.

We ourselves will be unable to overcome a listless tedium, or accept a sacrifice that has no immediate reward, or really 'lose' our present life, as Jesus did, unless, like him, we clearly understand and imaginatively see the resurrection of mankind, the renewal of human fellowship through the unity of all men welded in unalterable love for each other, together with our Lord, come again to live among them.

Paradise, yes paradise, the word we no longer dare to utter, paradise awaited and longed for, is an indispensable motive if we would live as Christians now and throughout every moment of our brief life. A life with no attraction, a life of sacrifice, poverty, and prayer, cut off from the passionate concerns of a materialistic society, would be an impossibility unless God and his paradise are awaited.

If we go on living without the expectation of this paradise, it may be because we are living on the surface of ourselves, tied unconsciously to some other reason for existence, to some transient attraction. But there are moments of truth, when choice becomes inescapable. Such moments may be rare occurrences in our life, but they shed a flood of light upon our real reasons for living and dying, and enable us to readjust our hope without allowing ourselves to be disconcerted by the impossibility of imagining the way in which the bodies of all men will rise again, and the nature of the society of the future as described in the Apocalypse. This is our belief. Come, Lord Jesus.

Luanda, 20 October

1960

I have had occasion to remark several times that when we say we have no time to pray, most often it has nothing to do with any lack of time, but with a kind of psychological impossibility to make use of the requisite time, due to an internal state of tension and turmoil. The question arises particularly with regard to those brief moments of prayer such as the saying of the *Angelus* or the *Veni Creator* in common, in the morning, before we start off to begin our various occupations during the day, when as the result of a timetable over concentrated on the morning, Mass has to be celebrated in the evening. Watch in hand, I have calculated that two and a half minutes would be sufficient for these two prayers to be said aloud. And yet I am told that in some Brotherhoods there is no time to say them! In reality we often spend more than two and a half minutes in settling some material problems or in exchanging a few words with a neighbour before leaving!

What really happens is this: we are inwardly in such turmoil that it is practically impossible to pause for a couple of minutes and keep calm and self-possessed. It is the existence of an inner state of mind like this, rather than the material omission of a short prayer, that is injurious. The majority of our fellow citizens are in this state of tension today. One has only to watch them walking to the gates of the underground!

The state of frantic hurry is wholly illogical and futile; it does not save time; quite the contrary. And yet we put ourselves in this position because we make no resistance to the pressure of a timetable, and the only reason for it that we admit is that it enables us to do more. This is an illusion. I am, of course, speaking about a state of subjective turmoil and not about sensible material arrangements that objectively try to prevent *a real waste of time*.

It is a state of mind the very opposite of that which is requisite for recollection. Since our vocation obliges us to find the way to contemplative prayer without giving up our human contacts, it is important for us to take measures to achieve [precisely] a condition of inward calm . . . I have known monks who were living in the noiseless, even rhythm of the cloister, and yet had troubled and tense souls; and on the other hand, there are men living in the world, over-burdened by work and anxieties, who manage to preserve a great inner calm. . . . We are frail beings. Even so, we are often responsible for not having taken the natural means—and this often means fidelity to very little things—to secure that human equilibrium which is the essential ground of contemplation. These may perhaps be only earth-bound foundations, but without them no ascent to God can become normal.

Why is this inner turmoil so common, and what causes it?

In the first place, we may be temperamentally predisposed to a state of tension of this kind, or it may result from past behaviour. We can improve our temperament with the help of God's grace, unwearying patience, humility, and perseverance. We should never look for immediate results, nor strain the psychological resources at our disposal at any given moment.

Secondly, we must reckon with the influence of our surroundings, with all their consequences of frayed nerves, overwork, and lack of sleep. In this sphere we certainly cannot always do everything we would like to, and we may well be satisfied if we do the most that duty makes obligatory in these circumstances.

But the most important and subtle cause of this imbalance very often lies within ourselves. We experience a feeling of frustration, of profound dissatisfaction, and we miss a happiness for which we hope. We do not dare to dwell on this, and with disinterested loyalty and a constantly tense determination, we strive to give ourselves to men and God in a spirit of radical self-denial that seems to us inhuman. What, then, is the truth of the matter? Are the religious life, the call to the apostolate, to an existence dedicated to God alone, really inhuman? And is such psychological tension the normal consequence of a decision to follow our Lord all the way to Calvary? Does it, in fact, mean that all tranquil happiness and every kind of deeply human fulfilment must be given up? And since this is an impossibility, our nature unconsciously rebels, and we are driven to support ourselves by a resolute but joyless loyalty. Is this not too frequently the fact? Many priests, monks, and lay apostles do in fact have a more or less muddled idea that this is how things are, but they do not dwell on the fact and fill their field of consciousness with as many other concerns as possible. They are afraid of solitude and of any prolonged recollection. The latter even seems impossible. It is as though one's spiritual life is a flimsy structure, liable to crash at a moment's pause for reflection, for that would reveal how profoundly unfulfilled we are.

In reality, however, the true following of our Lord cannot involve self-destruction. Where then does the error, if there is one, spring from? The saints in the past seem to have sounded a different note. It is true that they practised self-sacrifice, complete self-denial, but this was accompanied by a sense of fulfilment and peace. We have a confused awareness that in the spiritual circumstances of the world today there exists something impalpable, like a tendency, a more or less conscious predisposition to this pessimism, this despair that grips us.

I am thinking here of Christians only and not of materialists or existentialists for whom such a mental outlook is logical. For Christians are, in fact, in danger of adopting a false point of view, as the result of the more or less conscious acceptance of the common intellectual premises of an unbelieving world. The idea that is formed of Christian perfection, for instance, is dominated by a version of disinterested love of other people of such a nature that we come unconsciously to believe that it is an imperfection, to say the least, if we are not willing to accept complete physical, psychological, and spiritual exhaustion for their sake! We no longer dare to admit that we have an irresistible need for personal happiness and fulfilment. Dying from thirst for happiness that is all too real, we imagine for some reason that our Lord is asking us to be willing to give it up.

We feel a deep embarrassment, almost a complex, at having to admit our thirst for personal happiness, in the presence of those who, not without irony, proclaim the mythical and egotistic character of belief in the perfect happiness of another life. We come to think that we are more or less obliged to practice 'pure love', a form of love which claims to give up utterly and for ever all desire for personal satisfaction. All that is left is a life lived in a state in which proprietorship of one's own personality is renounced for the sake of one's neighbour, foreswearing as an imperfection, now overcome, that thirst for happiness which tormented us, and which we believe must be given up if we would attain perfect charity.

One fine day this bubble will burst, because we have reached the limit and can deny ourselves no longer. Having been unable to accept or await God's paradise, we are in danger of yielding to the first temptation that presents itself and entirely reduce desire to the level of a human love shared by two people only. To some this will even seem to be more disinterested and less egotistic than solitary chastity from which happiness is no longer expected.

A more or less explicit idea of this kind of 'pure love' underlies many a spiritual crisis. We may, indeed, ask whether it is not a kind of unconscious Christianisation of the Marxist false disinterestedness that considers that the greatness of the human ideal lies wholly in the sacrifice of our generation for the sake of the common benefit of those that come after, no claim to any personal reward being allowed . . .

The title of a recent book on the spiritual life, *Heaven is other people*, is a good example of this tendency. Just as it is lawful to emphasise the Christian imperatives bearing upon universal fraternal love, it is, on the other hand, erroneous and dangerous to appear to attribute to human beings, even considered as brothers whom Christ loves, that which belongs to the infinite being of God who alone can quench that thirst for the absolute and for happiness which is inherent in us all.

Christians must learn how to escape from this infection which is often very subtle and, in particular, gravely distorts the idea of the religious life. We must rediscover human equilibrium as created by God, and re-created by Christ, and we must have the courage to see God as the integral source of happiness and fulfilment for every man. The renunciation our Lord asks from us is not the abandonment of the essential desires of our nature but a temporary abstention from certain limited good things in order that we may more certainly obtain the unshakeable possession of a greater, a supreme good . . . So long as we have not accepted the need to find a more secure path to a greater happiness, as the ultimate motive for our religious life, we shall not have achieved the necessary conditions for complete spiritual equilibrium.

The miracle of our Lord is that he could offer himself to us as the source of happiness, and at the same time as the one who is most worthy of our love. His happiness therefore truly becomes our own; we can incorporate all things in his love, and this is the genuine 'pure love'. The cross is like a surgical operation which heals us and other men. We must pass through it with our gaze fixed beyond. We cannot do better than our Lord himself who was eager to have done with the agony in Gethsemane and the cross of Calvary, because he thirsted intensely for something different; for the end of suffering, for his resurrection and the glorification of his manhood.

Casablanca, 8 February